D1420738

26.8.67

Please read the pictures of this 1967 story clockwise — and, watch out — do not attempt to climb any watchtowers unless you are a time-served clock-repairer!

Printed and Published in Great Britain by
D. C. Thomson & Co., Ltd.,
185 Fleet Street, London, EC4A 2HS.
© D. C. THOMSON & CO., LTD., 2005.
ISBN 1 84535 040 5

(Certain stories do not appear exactly as originally published.)

A SPIN
ROUND
THE
SIXTIES
ZIP!

SPIN ROUND AND YOU'LL FIND:
DENNIS THE MENACE
DESPERATE DAN
ROGER THE DODGER
BASHSTREET KIDS
SONG HEAD
THE JOKER
THE BRIDE OF THE BEAR LORD
DIRTY DICK
SNEAKY PETE
THE PUPPY
THE CHEAT
THE PURPLE CLOUD
CRAZY CRAIG
OUTSIDER
FOR THE LOVER
TANK
THE THREE BEARS
THE WOODEN SUBMARINE
BILLY THE GOAT
BIG MAZZ
SMASHER
BEAR
HAUNTED
CHIPS
PEDDLER
CRAZY
THE CRIMSON BALL

'60s
THESE ARE AUTOMATIC TV TEACHERS. THEY COST VERY LITTLE TO HIRE.
BY JOVE! WHAT A GREAT INVENTION!
NEXT MORNING, THE NEW AUTOMATIC TEACHERS ARE FITTED –
RIGHT, CHILDREN! START DOING THE PROBLEMS AS THEY APPEAR ON THE SCREEN.
CRUMBS! WE'RE NOT TOO KEEN ON THIS. GOOD OLD TEACHER NEVER GAVE US HARD PROBLEMS LIKE THESE!
WHO DISCOVERED LIVERPOOL?
The BASH STREET SCHOOL 1964
I'LL EXPECT THE PROBLEMS TO BE ANSWERED WHEN I RETURN.
AW! HAVE A HEART, HEADMASTER!
SPELL "MARMALADE"
SUDDENLY –
BANG!
CLASS 1B
WHOOPEE!
YAHOO!
THIS IS SUPER!
THUNDER OF HOOVES
WHOOP!
BANG!
BANG!
BANG!
GOOD GRACIOUS! WHAT'S GOING ON?
TEE-HEE! WE SWITCHED OVER TO DIFFERENT CHANNELS.
BANG! BANG!
INSOLENT CHILD!
ON GUARD!
COME BACK HERE–ERK!
TRIP
SMASH!
CRASH!
CRUMP!
TEE-HEE! WE'LL JUST TAKE THE REST OF THE DAY OFF. THE TV TEACHERS DO LOOK ILL!
GROAN! THAT INVENTION DIDN'T WORK! NEVER MIND — THERE'S STILL CCTV, BUBBLE CARS, WEATHER PREDICTIONS AND SPACE CAPSULES TO SEE . . . BUT WE'LL START OFF WITH A PIANO AND A HORSE! TURN THE PAGE, PLEASE!
22.2.64

MY AUNT HAS REMOVED FROM THIS HOUSE, BUT SHE LEFT A FEW THINGS BEHIND, AND THICK HEAD AND I ARE FOLLOWING ON WITH THEM.
GASP! WHEEZE! WHEW! I'LL NEVER GET THIS HEAVY CABINET DOWNSTAIRS!
HUH! IT WOULDN'T EVEN GO THROUGH THE BEDROOM DOOR! BUT THAT OLD BEDSTEAD ON THE PATHWAY MIGHT SOLVE THE PROBLEM!
WITH A MIGHTY HEAVE, THICK HEAD LAUNCHES THE CABINET OVER THE WINDOW-SILL—
HEE-HEE! I WONDER HOW THAT FAT SAP'S GETTING ON UP THERE WITH THAT HEAVY CABINET? IT'S MADE OF SOLID—
ZOO-OOM
BOUNCE
THUD
BIG HEAD and THICK HEAD
AND SO, AFTER REMOVING THE UPSTAIRS WINDOW-FRAME—
THAT'S THE HORSE HARNESSED! NOW TO LOWER THE PIANO ON TO THE CART WITH THIS INGENIOUS PULLEY SYSTEM I'VE INVENTED!
LOWER AWAY!
10 MINUTES LATER—
HERE WE ARE! I'VE BORROWED THE MILKMAN'S HORSE. WE'LL BACK IT INTO THE SHAFTS, AND IT'LL PULL THE LOAD EASILY—PIANO AND ALL!
GOSH! WHAT BRAINS!
WOW! THE ROPES HAVE SNAPPED!
AGH-H! WHAT'S HAPPENED?
WHOOSH
15 MINUTES LATER, PASSERS-BY SEE A FANTASTIC SIGHT—
'60S
6.6.64

In the dim and distant past — that is, The Dandy, 1964, when horses pulled carts and everyone had solid mahogany wardrobes in their bedrooms and upright pianos in their sitting rooms, a certain dim pair were never too distant from trouble!
POIN-NG
—MAHOGANY!
BLAH-H!
WHEE-EE
SHATTERING CRASH
HALF AN HOUR LATER—WHEN BIG HEAD HAS REGAINED CONSCIOUSNESS—
BAH! HE'S MAKING ME WORK DOWN HERE TO KEEP ME OUT OF TROUBLE! CALLED ME A FAT NIT! BUT I'LL SHOW HIM! I'LL SHIFT THE STAIR CARPET ALL BY MYSELF! HERE GOES!
—AGH-H-H-H H!
WHIZZ
TUG
TWO HOURS LATER—WHEN THICK HEAD HAS RECOVERED HIS MEAGRE SUPPLY OF SCATTERED WITS—
PHEW! I CAN'T BUDGE THE CART AN INCH, AND THE PIANO HAS TO GO ON YET!
POOH! MY SUPERIOR INTELLIGENCE WORKED OUT THAT PROBLEM HOURS AGO! LEAVE IT TO ME!
EE-YULK! —NO!
YOU BLITHERING, HALF-BAKED, BRAINLESS BLOCKHEAD! DIDN'T YOU SEE ME UP THERE?
OKAY, BRAINY—BONCE! SO, YOU GOT THE PERISHING PIANO ON WHAT'S LEFT OF THE CART! ALL I WANT TO KNOW NOW IS, HOW DO WE GET THE BLITHERING HORSE OFF THE BLOOMING ROOF?

'60s
The bubble-car was one of the icons of the '60s — as was Biffo the Bear! Put the two together and you get . . . er . . . a caravan on fire!
LET'S MAKE SOME CHIPS FOR SUPPER TONIGHT.
WE'VE GOT PLENTY OF COOKING FAT!
BIFFO THE BEAR
HELP! THE PLACE IS ON FIRE!
MUST CALL THE FIRE BRIGADE!
TELEPHONE
TELEPHONE
OUT OF ORDER
PUFF! THAT HOUSE WILL HAVE A TELEPHONE! GASP!
OH, NO!
GONE ON HOLIDAY
THERE'S ONLY ONE THING FOR IT!
FIRE BRIGADE
BRRING!
RING!
FIRE BRIGADE
WELL, THAT'S THE FIRST TIME I'VE HEARD OF A FIRE GOING TO THE FIRE BRIGADE!
CHIEF
6.10.62

Poor Professor Screwtop's hopes for a successful weather rocket lift-off were laughed off by Snooty and his pals — but it was Snooty and his pals who were soon to be in hot water . . .

Throw one bald Head and one jaded Teacher into a well-used school, add a sprinkling of Kids, mix well for two pages . . . a perfect recipe for laughter! School dinners have moved on since this Bash Street Kids story — but not all of them were thrown across the tables!

I WANT MY PUDDING!
HERE, TAKE MINE- IT'S 'ORRIBLE!

THEN-
DIRECT PIPELINE FROM SOUP POT
SLOP!
BURP!
DISGUSTIN' MANNERS.
GOT THAT FLY!
SLABBER!
SLURP!
GOBBLE!
HELP!
'S TOO HOT!
BREEZE
CLINK
SLOO!
SLURP!
BURP!
BOP!

TUT! TUT! THEIR TABLE MANNERS ARE DISGUSTING. YOU MUST SEE THAT THEY IMPROVE BECAUSE I'VE INVITED THE SCHOOL GOVERNORS TO LUNCHEON TOMORROW.
SCHOOL PUD

THAT NIGHT, DANNY HOLDS A SUMMIT CONFERENCE ON TOP OF THE SLAG-HEAP.
COR! I DIDN'T THINK THEY'D BE WORKIN' OVERTIME. NEVER MIND, WE'LL HAVE SOME FUN AT THE GOVERNORS' LUNCHEON TOMORROW. NOW HERE'S WHAT WE'LL DO, BZZZ....

NEXT DAY AT THE GOVERNORS' LUNCHEON-
AH, I'M GLAD TO SEE THAT THE CHILDREN ARE ON THEIR BEST BEHAVIOUR.
WHAT WELL-BEHAVED PUPILS! ALL I NEED NOW IS A GOOD MEAL.
TEACHER'S PLACE
GOLDEN SILENCE
SMUG

I'LL CARVE THE TURKEY NOW. OOPS! WHERE HAS DANNY GONE TO?
GONE
HISS
HISS
JAB

DISGUSTING EXHIBITION! WE'LL CUT THE MASTERS' FOOD ALLOWANCE FOR THAT, AND WE SHAN'T LET YOU NEAR THE KIDS' FOOD EITHER.
YOU'LL HEAR MORE ABOUT THIS INCIDENT. GOOD DAY!
SNIGGER

SO THE GOVERNORS EMPLOY FRED CRUMPET, THE CHEF FROM THE RITZ HOTEL, TO COOK FOR THE KIDS.
CAN I HAVE A TENTH HELPING OF PUD, PLEASE?
CHOMP
CHOMP
YUM YUM
CERTAINLY.
BREAD AND WATER! UGH!
WATER
MASTERS' ALLOWANCE
60s

'60s
Children drink too much fruit juice . . .
And eat too many sweets . . .
JOE'S SODA FOUNTAIN
FIZZY FRUITO DRINKS SATISFY
SHLUP! THOSE FIZZY-FRUITOS ARE - GLUG! SMASHIN'!
ASSISTANT WANTED
SLURP!
SUCK!
FIZZY FRUITO DRINKS
JOE'S SODA FOUNTAIN
FATTY BEING A GROWING LAD, NEEDS THREE DRINKS.
SHLLOO!
SMIFFY, OF COURSE ALWAYS DOES THINGS WRONG—
SPLOOSH!
OUTSIDE.
TUT! TUT! YOU MUST CEASE DRINKING THAT FOUL BREW. I'LL GIVE YOU A LESSON ON DIET!
SPLAT!
SPLUT!
SPLUT!
BONK! BONK!
JAB!
IN CLASS
NOW PAY ATTENTION TO WHAT I'VE DRAWN HERE!
BREAD + CHEESE
GOOD
BAD
FIZZY FRUITO DRINK
NUTS TO YOU— GLUG! — TEACHER!
SLOO!
SHLUP!
Z-Z-Z
SO TEACHER BEGINS TO THINK—
AH! I KNOW HOW TO STOP THEM GUZZLING FIZZY FRUITO!
NEXT POCKET-MONEY DAY—
YIPPEE! FIZZY FRUITOS HERE WE COME!
JOE'S SODA FOUNTAIN
YOU'RE NEW HERE, AREN'T YOU? WELL WE ALWAYS DRINK FIZZY FRUITOS, SO POUR 'EM OUT!
FIZZY FRUITOS THEY'RE LOVELY
HERE YOU ARE, KIDS.
SUCK!
DEEP BREATHS!
J-A-A-AH!
SLURP!
SHLOO!
BLARGH!
ECCH!
GROOOH!
GET YOUR FIZZY FRUITO DRINKS AT JOE'S SODA FOUNTAIN
GROOO! WE'LL NEVER TOUCH THAT HORRIBLE STUFF AGAIN!
I PROMISE NEVER TO DR
HEH! HEH! I SIGNED ON AS ASSISTANT FOR THE DAY. I THOUGHT THAT A SPOT OF CASTOR OIL IN THE FIZZY FRUITO WOULD FIX THE KIDS!
CASTOR OIL
27.1.62

Hasn't Dirty Dick heard of automatic washer/driers? Well, no, 'cos it was all manual labour in 1967!

No, they're not modern health hazard messages...
They're forty-year-old
Bash Street Kids pages!
THIS IS MR GNASHER, THE SCHOOLS' DENTAL INSPECTOR. HE'S HERE TO EXAMINE YOUR TEETH!
MUNCH!
CHOMP!
JELLY BABIES
LIQUORICE STICKS
HUM BUGS
FIRST, WE WILL DISPOSE OF THESE FOUL THINGS— THEY ARE BAD FOR YOUR TEETH!
MINTS
TOFFEES
WASTE
IF YOU WANT GOOD TEETH, EAT PLENTY OF APPLES AND CARROTS —
SWEETS
GOOD
BAD
DO HAVE A SWEET, MR GNASHER, SIR!
MR GNASHER CONTINUES —
— AND REMEMBER TO CLEAN YOUR TEETH AT LEAST TWICE A DAY!
TOOTH PASTE
YIPPEE! THE BELL! TIME TO GO HOME —ERK!
D-DING!
REMEMBER - I WANT TO SEE AN IMPROVEMENT NEXT WEEK —
—OR ELSE!
SO THE KIDS SET ABOUT IMPROVING THEIR TEETH.
SORRY, FRED, BUT I NEED THAT CARROT!
SNATCH!
FRED
I MUST GET UP A NICE SHINE ON BOTH OF MY TEETH FOR THE INSPECTION!
GLOSS SPRAY POLISH
RUB!
EAT PLENTY OF APPLES — BURP! — HE SAID!
12 lbs APPLES
THEN —
AH! VERY GOOD! I'M SURE MR GNASHER WILL BE PLEASED TOMORROW!
SUN GLASSES!
GLEAM!
DAZZLING SMILE!
NEVER BE WITHOUT A BEAND
NEXT DAY ON THE WAY TO SCHOOL —
LET'S CHALLENGE THOSE BASH ST DRIPS TO A FIGHT, YAH! WE DON'T LIKE YOU!
CLONK!
SLOB STREET SCHOOL
THE CHALLENGE IS ACCEPTED —
WE DON'T LIKE YOU EITHER! —UGH!
THUMP!
BASH!
ZONK!
CRUNCH!
AT THE TOOTH INSPECTION —
PROUD
LET MR GNASHER SEE YOUR TEETH, CHILDREN!
GASHP!
HERE THEY ARE MR GNASHER! THOSHE ROTTEN SHLOB SHTREET BOYSH KNOCKED 'EM ALL OUT!
CLATTER!
17. 2. 62

JONAH

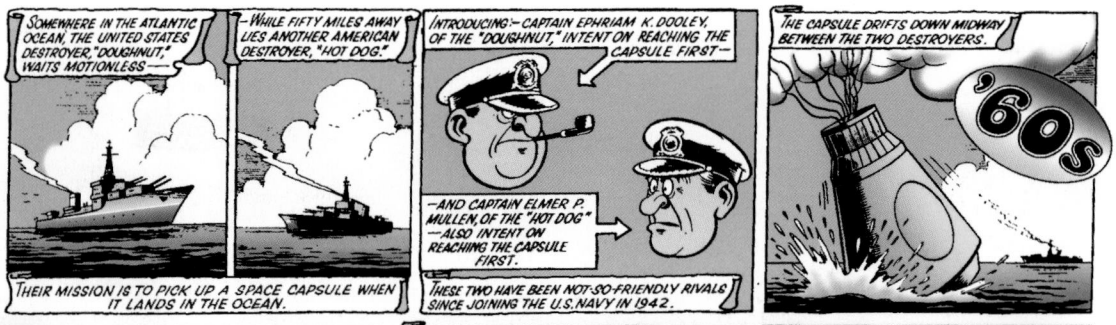

Astronaut John Glenn was in orbit round the Earth in February 1962. Four months later, in The Beano, it looked as if the only safe place for naval nitwit Jonah might be in space, too!

2.6.62

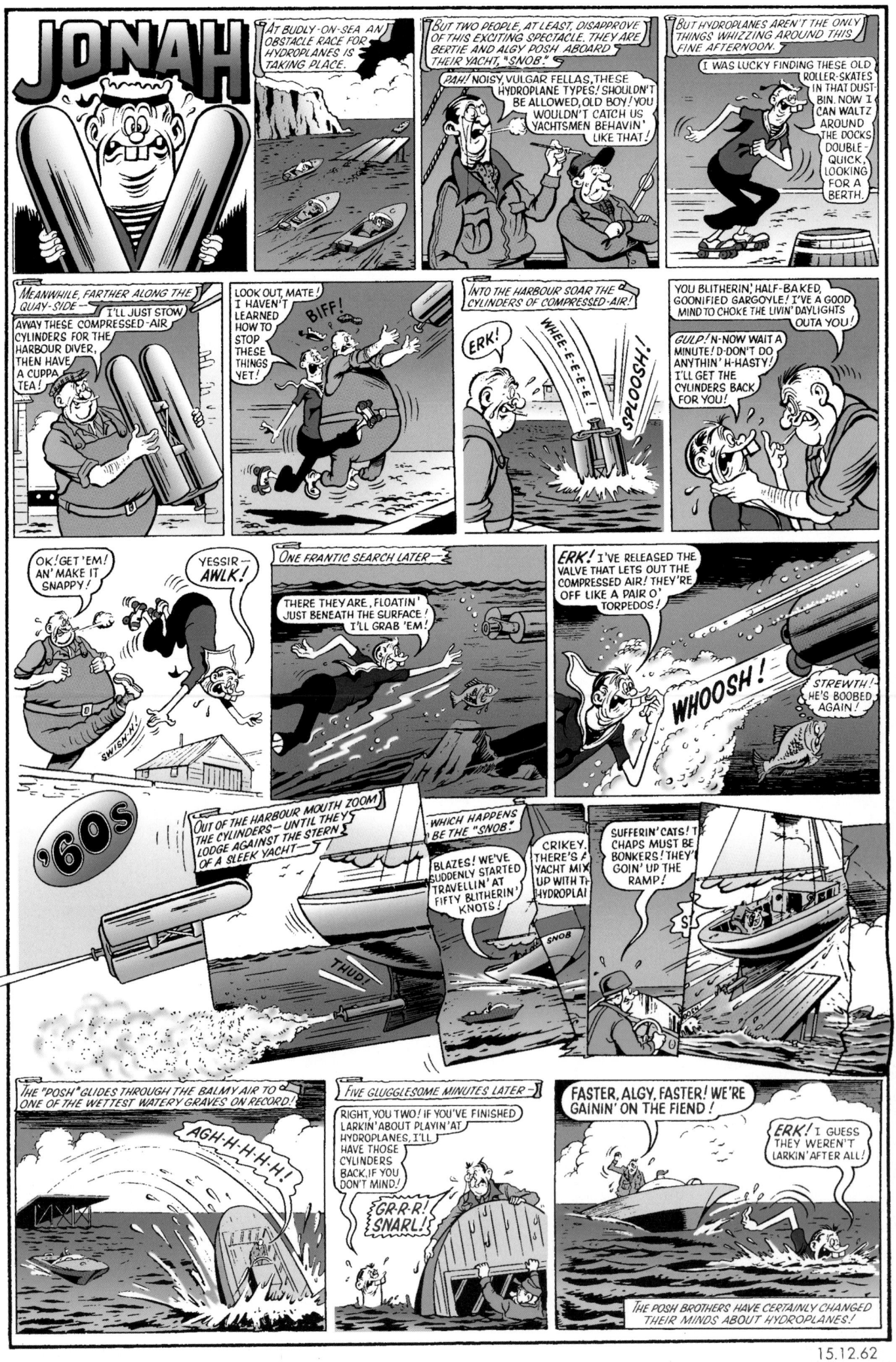
JONAH
AT BUDLY-ON-SEA AN OBSTACLE RACE FOR HYDROPLANES IS TAKING PLACE.
BUT TWO PEOPLE, AT LEAST, DISAPPROVE OF THIS EXCITING SPECTACLE. THEY ARE BERTIE AND ALGY POSH ABOARD THEIR YACHT, "SNOB."
PAH! NOISY, VULGAR FELLAS, THESE HYDROPLANE TYPES! SHOULDN'T BE ALLOWED, OLD BOY! YOU WOULDN'T CATCH US YACHTSMEN BEHAVIN' LIKE THAT!
BUT HYDROPLANES AREN'T THE ONLY THINGS WHIZZING AROUND THIS FINE AFTERNOON.
I WAS LUCKY FINDING THESE OLD ROLLER-SKATES IN THAT DUST-BIN. NOW I CAN WALTZ AROUND THE DOCKS DOUBLE-QUICK, LOOKING FOR A BERTH.
MEANWHILE, FARTHER ALONG THE QUAY-SIDE—
I'LL JUST STOW AWAY THESE COMPRESSED-AIR CYLINDERS FOR THE HARBOUR DIVER, THEN HAVE A CUPPA TEA!
LOOK OUT, MATE! I HAVEN'T LEARNED HOW TO STOP THESE THINGS YET!
BIFF!
INTO THE HARBOUR SOAR THE CYLINDERS OF COMPRESSED-AIR!
ERK!
WHEE-E-E-E-E!
SPLOOSH!
YOU BLITHERIN', HALF-BAKED, GOONIFIED GARGOYLE! I'VE A GOOD MIND TO CHOKE THE LIVIN' DAYLIGHTS OUTA YOU!
GULP! N-NOW WAIT A MINUTE! D-DON'T DO ANYTHIN' H-HASTY! I'LL GET THE CYLINDERS BACK FOR YOU!
OK! GET 'EM! AN' MAKE IT SNAPPY!
YESSIR— AWLK!
SWISH-H!
ONE FRANTIC SEARCH LATER—
THERE THEY ARE, FLOATIN' JUST BENEATH THE SURFACE! I'LL GRAB 'EM!
ERK! I'VE RELEASED THE VALVE THAT LETS OUT THE COMPRESSED AIR! THEY'RE OFF LIKE A PAIR O' TORPEDOS!
WHOOSH!
STREWTH! HE'S BOOBED AGAIN!
'60S
OUT OF THE HARBOUR MOUTH ZOOM THE CYLINDERS— UNTIL THEY LODGE AGAINST THE STERN OF A SLEEK YACHT—
THUD!
WHICH HAPPENS TO BE THE "SNOB."
BLAZES! WE'VE SUDDENLY STARTED TRAVELLIN' AT FIFTY BLITHERIN' KNOTS!
CRIKEY. THERE'S A YACHT MIX UP WITH TH HYDROPLAI
SNOB
SUFFERIN' CATS! T CHAPS MUST BE BONKERS! THEY' GOIN' UP THE RAMP!
S
THE "POSH" GLIDES THROUGH THE BALMY AIR TO ONE OF THE WETTEST WATERY GRAVES ON RECORD!
AGH-H-H-H-H!
FIVE GLUGGLESOME MINUTES LATER—
RIGHT, YOU TWO! IF YOU'VE FINISHED LARKIN' ABOUT PLAYIN' AT HYDROPLANES, I'LL HAVE THOSE CYLINDERS BACK, IF YOU DON'T MIND!
GR-R-R! SNARL!
FASTER, ALGY, FASTER! WE'RE GAININ' ON THE FIEND!
ERK! I GUESS THEY WEREN'T LARKIN' AFTER ALL!
THE POSH BROTHERS HAVE CERTAINLY CHANGED THEIR MINDS ABOUT HYDROPLANES!

15.12.62

Computers have changed beyond all recognition since this story was printed in 1969 — but Lord Snooty looked the same for over 25 years!

The first series of Brassneck appeared in the Dandy from 5.12.64 right through to 24.2.68. There are "signs" of laughter in the episode below, when Charlie and his metal pal slip into "mirth" gear on their bikes!

BRASSNECK

FIZZ! Chuckler Charley Brand and his metal pal, Brassneck, groaned with dismay. The front tyre of Charley's bicycle had been punctured.

HEY, LOOK, BRASSNECK! IT'S FIVE-TO-NINE. I'LL BE LATE FOR SCHOOL.

OH, DEAR!

Brassneck leapt into action. Balancing the bicycle on its back wheel, he pedalled along like mad.

YIPPEE! KEEP IT UP, BRASSNECK!

But as the bicycle zipped round the corner into the playground, it ran slap-bang into Fatso Snodgrass, Charley's teacher.

OOYAH!

OOF!

Fatso was most annoyed about being run over—and he meant to do something about it.

YOU'RE A SET OF RECKLESS CLOTS ON BICYCLES. I'M GOING TO TAKE YOU DOWN TO THE ROAD SAFETY CENTRE THIS MORNING FOR SOME PRACTICE!

At the road safety centre, Fatso began by giving a demonstration of safe cycling.

NOW WATCH ME CAREFULLY AS I PREPARE TO TURN LEFT.

WITH A BIT OF LUCK, MAYBE HE'LL FALL OFF!

Meanwhile, Brassneck had gone looking for a cycle of his own—and he found one.

Z-BICYCLE REPORTING TO H.Q. I'M KEEPING A LOOK OUT FOR BILL THE BICYCLE THIEF!

The metal lad leapt on the bobby's bike and cycled off.

EMERGENCY CALL TO H.Q.! SOMEONE HAS JUST STOLEN MY Z-BICYCLE!

Constable Higgins dashed around raising the alarm. Soon from every quarter, cops were speeding to his assistance.

THERE HE GOES! CATCH HIM!

I'M OFF!

HELP!

EEK!

OOF!

YIPPEE! GOOD OLD FATSO! HE DID FALL OFF!

Brassneck was followed back to the road safety centre by hordes of bobbies. What an uproar! The bobbies sped hither and thither round the circuit, ignoring all the road signs and giving no signals. Poor Fatso was sent flying by one of the flying squad. Brassneck took advantage of the uproar to nip over the wall.

Constable Higgins' bike had been recovered– but Fatso Snodgrass had also recovered– and he was blazing.
YOU RECKLESS NITWITS! WHAT'S THE IDEA?
The furious Fatso gave the abashed bobbies a real dressing down.
AND IN FUTURE, YOU'LL OBEY ALL THE ROAD SIGNS HERE—OR I'LL REPORT YOU TO THE POLICE!
Not far off, Brassneck had given up hope of borrowing a bicycle, and was planning to build one!
THIS IS JUST WHAT I'M LOOKING FOR!
RUBBISH DUMP
The metal lad constructed a super bike. But there was one odd thing about it. He had to pedal with his hands and steer with his feet! And he could only do that upside down and looking backwards!
AH-HA! NOW HERE'S A ROUND ABOUT. I'VE GOT TO KEEP TO MY LEFT.
In this position, it was difficult for Brassneck to read road signs correctly. And when the metal boy approached a "Keep Left" sign he forgot he was upside down and he turned to HIS left! Which was actually the right – and that, of course, was wrong!
KEEP LEFT
What a mix-up Brassneck caused!
HAWKHILL FLYOVER
TUNNEL TRAFFIC ONE-WAY
M-106 SLIPWAY
KEEP LEFT
BENSHIE BY-PASS
WOW! HE'S GIVEN ME THE SLIP AGAIN!
Cars and lorries smashed into one another. Buses swerved off the road. Soon every traffic cop in the district was chasing the tin-can boy. And in the end Brassneck himself had to make a quick turn off the road to get away from it all!
GOSH! HE'S LANDED ON SOMEONE!
WOW!
OOF!
Brassneck's bicycle went careering over an embankment and crashed down on a cyclist passing along the road below.
Despite all the damage he had done, Brassneck was congratulated for bringing about the arrest of the very man the police had been hunting so long!
WELL I NEVER! IT'S BILL THE BICYCLE THIEF!
WELL DONE, LADDIE!

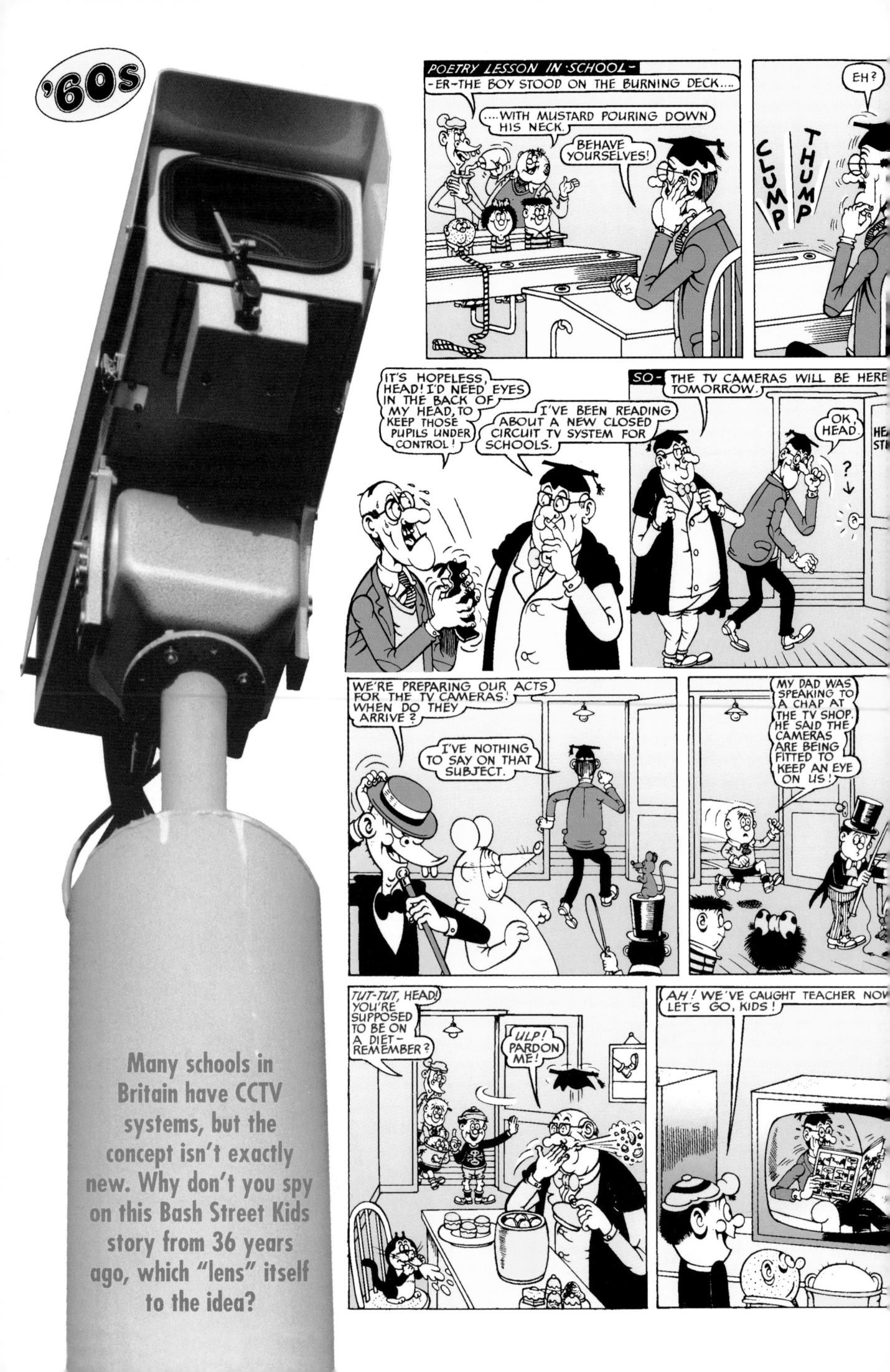

Many schools in Britain have CCTV systems, but the concept isn't exactly new. Why don't you spy on this Bash Street Kids story from 36 years ago, which "lens" itself to the idea?

WHAT ON EARTH ARE YOU TWO DOING?
WE WERE JUST LIBERATING OUR MOUSE!
CONFISCATED
ERK! WHAT'S THAT COMMOTION NOW?
I'D KNOCK SPOTS OFF YOU IF ONLY I COULD SEE YOU!
I NEVER HIT A BOY WITH GLASSES - BUT IN YOUR CASE I'LL MAKE AN EXCEPTION!
GET BACK TO YOUR DESKS OR I'LL KNOCK SPOTS OFF BOTH OF YOU!
THE TV CAMERAS ARE COMING! THIS IS OUR CHANCE TO BE GREAT STARS
AT LAST!
HOW'S THAT, TEACHER?
HOW ABOUT THIS, TEACHER?
HEY, KID! WHERE ARE THOSE CAMERAS SUPPOSED TO BE?
ONE IN THE STAFF ROOM, AND ONE IN THE HEAD'S STUDY!
HEH-HEH! WE CAN KEEP AN EYE ON THE STAFF! LET'S GO TO THE HEAD'S STUDY!
AH-AH! NAUGHTY TEACHER! YOU'RE SUPPOSED TO BE CORRECTING OUR EXAM PAPERS!
BEANO
SOME TIME LATER-
LOVELY CAMERAS! GET YOUR TV CAMERAS HERE! HARDLY USED!
8.11.69

Here's a tip for all the Beano and Dandy readers! Actually there are **two** tips, one in each story . . . make that **three**, including the background picture! Anyway, the tip is . . . always separate your rubbish into recyclable and non-recyclable, unless your name is Dirty Dick! As for Dennis, it was a rubbish idea to hide in that cloud of smoke anyway!

DENNIS the MENACE
3.12.66
GENTLE SPLASH!
TEE-HEE! SUCH FUN!
SURELY YOU'RE NOT GOING TO LET WALTER OFF WITH THAT, DENNIS?
I CERTAINLY AM NOT!
INK
LATER–
TEE-HEE! SUCH FUN!
THEN–
HERE'S A PRESENT FOR YOU, DEAR– A WATER-RIFLE.
OH, THANK YOU, DADDY! THIS'LL FIX NASTY DENNIS!
SO–
ONE UP TO ME!
SPLOOSH!
ONE UP TO HIM, EH? WE'LL SEE ABOUT THAT!
HEH! HEH! C-CRUMBS! WHO'S THAT BEHIND WALTER?
WHOOSH!
IT'S DENNIS'S DAD!
COME HERE AT ONCE, BOY!
RUBBISH
SNIGGER! DAD'LL NEVER FIND ME IN THIS SMOKE SCREEN!
WE'D BETTER PUT OUT THAT FIRE ON THE DUMP, CLARENCE.
CHUCKLE! SUPER DODGE, THIS!
AH! THERE YOU ARE!
WHOOSH!
AHA! I KNOW THE BEST WAY TO DRY YOU OFF AND STOP YOU CATCHING A CHILL!
LATER–
HUH! I'D RATHER HAVE HAD A CHILL!
BETTER COOL THIS DOWN NOW!

'G FOR GIANT', from The Beano of 1962, could have been seen a

a warning for the future, and its message is still relevant today.

There may have been "Three Steps To Heaven" according to Eddie Cochran, back in 1960's music charts, but Minnie the Minx found **her** set of steps led to disaster!

1 THREE STEPS TO HEAVEN Eddie Cochran

MINNIE THE MINX
YOU REALLY MUST KEEP MINNIE OUT OF MISCHIEF, DAD.
RIGHT! I'LL GIVE HER A JOB TO DO.
SO, SNEAKING OUT TO PLAY, EH?.... COME BACK THIS INSTANT! I WANT YOU TO RETURN THE SET OF STEPS I BORROWED FROM MR WILSON LAST WEEK.
WELL, IF IT ISN'T PERCY POTT, THE LITTLE BOY WHO'S ALWAYS RUNNING AWAY FROM ME!
OOH!
HEH! HEH! HE THINKS HE'S SAFE FROM ME BEHIND HIS HIGH GARDEN FENCE -
POTT
- BUT HE ISN'T!
I'VE GOT YOU THIS TIME, PERCY!
DADDY! DADDY! LET ME IN!
KNOCK! KNOCK!
AARGH!
ZOOM!
SPLUT!
EVEN WHEN CARRYING A SET OF STEPS, I'M STILL A GOOD SPRINTER!
GRR!
HMM! I'VE JUST THOUGHT OF A WAY TO MAKE MONEY WITH THESE STEPS!
SO-
ROLL UP, KIDS! GET A SUPER VIEW OF THE MATCH! ONLY A PENNY EACH!
CUP-TIE ROVERS v UNITED
PLAY UP, THE ROVERS!
SUDDENLY-
CRASH!
ER-HERE ARE YOUR STEPS, MR WILSON!
AARGH!
BACK HOME -
MR POTT AND MR WILSON HAVE JUST BEEN ON THE 'PHONE TO ME. GO UP TO YOUR ROOM - I'M GOING TO TAKE STEPS TO SEE THAT YOU DON'T BOTHER ANYBODY FOR A WEEK!

THE Beano AND Dandy TOP TEN FROM THE '60s

One of Petula Clark's many hits in the Sixties was "Sailor". Did Beano readers at the time think she was singing about their favourite nautical nincompoop — Jonah — when she sang "Sailor, leave the sea"?

JONAH

2 SAILOR Petula Clark

ITS OWNER IS A PRODUCER OF UNDERWATER FILMS—HANS OFFE, WHO, WITH HIS WIFE, DOTTY, IS PLANNING TO MAKE A FILM, ENTITLED:—'EXPLORING SUNKEN WRECKS'.
TODAY, VE LOCATE ZER WRECK, MINE FRIEND, UND TOMORROW VE START ZER FILMING!
OKEYDOKE, MISTER OFFE!
SO HANS OFFE AND DOTTY TAKE THE PLUNGE TO LOCATE A SUNKEN WRECK!
AS THEY SUBMERGE, JONAH SURFACES!
COO! WHAT A SMASHING YACHT!
TEE-TUM-TI-TEE—ERK!
HARPOONED BY DOTTY (AGE 12)
WHEW! FOR ONE HORRIBLE SECOND I THOUGHT IT WAS THE BOSUN!
BOSUNS ALWAYS GREET ME WITH AN EXPRESSION LIKE THAT, Y'KNOW. I CAN'T THINK WHY!
THAT FACE LOOKS FAMILIAR, TOO!
MEXICAN FIEND
NABBED BY HANS—SINGLE 'ANDED.
THIS OLD TUB IS MORE LIKE A MUSEUM THAN A SHIP!
SUFFERIN' CATFISH! I'M GLAD THAT HORRIBLE, FIENDISH THING AIN'T ALIVE!
ORFUL NOSE-CRUNCHING CRAYFISH. (CHINA)
AGH-H-H-H-H! IT IS!
VORACIOUS WOOD-EATING TEREDO WORMS
AND SO ARE THESE!
ERK! AGH! ERK! OWCH!
MUNCH! CRUNCH! MUNCH! CRUNCH!
SLURP!!
NIP!
GETTITOFF!
HALF AN HOUR LATER—20 FATHOMS DOWN—
ACH! GOOT! AT LAST—ZER PERFECT WRECK FOR ZER FILM! A RECENT SINKING TOO, I SHOULD THINK!
HANS OFFE AND DOTTY SWIM ABOARD—
STRANGE! ISS VUN MASS OFF HOLES! ZIS ISS VER' INTERESTINK!
HANS! ZER CABIN! ZERE ISS SOMESING IN ZERE! OPEN ZER DOOR!
OYLK! GLOYLK! GLURK! EE-YULK!
ISS IMPOSSIBLE!
AGH-H! DOTTY! DON'T LOOK! ISS HORRIBLE!
GLEWK! GET THIS GLUGGLE OFF MY GLUG—GLUG! GLOOP—GLOYLK!
AWLK!
HANS! ZER SHIP ISS OURS!
HIMMEL!
DASCHUND
MEANWHILE—ON THE SURFACE—
I MUST GET TO A CHINESE, NOSE-CRUNCHING, CRAYFISH REMOVER BEFORE THESE PESKY, VORACIOUS, WOOD-EATING TEREDO WORMS GUZZLE MY OAR!
CRUNCH! MUNCH! MUNCH! CRUNCH!

3
MINNIE THE Minx
INTRODUCING OUR NEW SCHOOLGIRL SINGING STAR, WINNIE WARBLE, WHOSE LATEST SONG IS NOW AT THE TOP OF THE HIT PARADE....
GOSH! WISH I COULD GET ON THE HIT PARADE!
LITTLE MINX MUFFET SAT ON A PUFFET
NOW, GIRLS AND BOYS, WE NEED A FEW MORE VOICES IN THE SCHOOL CHOIR. I'LL TRY YOU OUT ONE AT A TIME — YOU FIRST, MINNIE!
OH, GOODY! THIS MAY BE THE FIRST STEP ON THE ROAD TO THE HIT PARADE!
I'LL SERENADE HIM AT HIS WINDOW. HE'S SURE TO REALISE I'VE GOT A GOOD VOICE!
YOWL!
SCREECH!
THE FEBRUARY
THESE CATS ARE A PEST! CLEAR OUT, YOU BRUTES!
WELL, THEY CAN'T ALL BE WRONG. I'LL STAY OFF SCHOOL AND GET SOME PRACTISE OUT IN THE COUNTRY AIR.
WAIL!
THAT WAS WONDERFUL, GIRLIE! COULD YOU DO IT AGAIN SO THAT I CAN RECORD IT?
WHY, CERTAINLY!
HIT PARADE, HERE I COME!
AH! THAT'S IT — A PERFECT IMITATION OF THE BALD-HEADED BLUEBIRD'S MORNING SONG!
WARBLE!
WAIL!

THE Beano AND Dandy TOP TEN FROM THE '60s

DON'T TREAT ME LIKE A CHILD Helen Shapiro

By 1962, songs like the above broke records for teenage sensation Helen Shapiro — two Number One hits and three others in the Top Five before she was sixteen years old. Minnie the Minx's voice could only break glass . . .

THE Beano AND Dandy TOP TEN FROM THE '60s

4 DISTANT DRUMS Jim Reeves

The velvet-voiced Mr Jim Reeves had a Number One Hit with "Distant Drums" in 1964. In the same year, Lord Snooty's pals wished that Snooty had distant drums too, as they did their best to get rid of them!

THE Beano AND Dandy
TOP TEN FROM THE '60s
DENNIS
5
DO WAH DIDDY DIDDY Manfred Mann
Manfred Mann's chart topping hit of 1964, "Do Wah Diddy Diddy", sums up this "baby" Dennis story from the same year, where Dad locks Dennis in a pram to keep him out of mischief. Maybe Dennis should re-title the song "Do What? Didn't! Didn't!"
THUMP!

the MENACE
YOUR SON'S BEEN MISBEHAVING AGAIN! CAN'T YOU DO SOMETHING TO KEEP HIM OUT OF TROUBLE?
WE'LL TRY, OFFICER!
THEY'RE ALWAYS PICKING ON ME.
LATER—
OH, YES, TOMMY'S A LITTLE RASCAL, BUT HE CAN'T GET UP TO ANY MISCHIEF WHEN HE'S STRAPPED IN HIS PRAM.
HMM!
SNARL!
BACK HOME—
WE'VE GOT TO THINK OF SOME WAY OF KEEPING DENNIS OUT OF TROUBLE.
DON'T WORRY, MY DEAR! I'VE THOUGHT OF A CUNNING PLAN.
SO—
WELL, DENNIS, WHAT DO YOU THINK OF YOUR PRAM?
MY PRAM? YOU'RE JOKING, OF COURSE!
I AM NOT! GET IN YOUR PRAM AT ONCE!
LET ME OUT! I'M NO INFANT!
DON'T WORRY, MUM. HE WON'T GET UP TO MISCHIEF NOW.
GRRR!
LOCKED IN.
DOWN THE STREET—
WHAT A DEAR LITTLE BABY! HERE'S A RATTLE FOR YOU.
COO! TA!
OOYAH!
ME HIT DADA!
I'LL MAKE HIM WISH HE'D NEVER GOT THIS PRAM.
RATTLE!
OH, DEAR!
YAROOP!
SNIGGER!
WHIZZ!
CRUNCH!
AT THE CROSS-ROADS—
WOW!
THUMP!
INNOCENCE
WHO'S IN CHARGE OF THIS RUNAWAY PRAM?
MY DADA THERE IN THE RED SUIT!
YOUR HUSBAND HAS BEEN UP TO MISCHIEF NOW—DRIVING A PRAM RECKLESSLY!
GRRR! YOU'LL FEEL THIS RATTLE LATER, BOY!
GROAN! WHAT A FAMILY! THEY'RE BOTH MENACES!
SUCK
12.12.64

THE Beano AND Dandy TOP TEN FROM THE '60s

Was Desperate Dan thinking of Marianne Faithfull's 1965 Top Ten hit "This Little Bird" when he was looking for someone to blame for this chaos back in 1969?

6 **THIS LITTLE BIRD** **Marianne Faithfull**

THE Beano AND Dandy
TOP TEN FROM THE '60s
Can you quickly identify the characters from their puppet parts in this figure? Answers below —
ANSWERS:—
Lord Snooty's head.
Body — Pa Bear.
Right arm —
Minnie the Minx.
Left Arm —
Dennis the Menace.
Right leg —
Biffo the Bear.
Left leg —
Billy Whizz.

Sandie Shaw's Eurovision Song Contest winning song in 1967, "PUPPET ON A STRING", was in the charts for over four months. In that same year, the Beano didn't have a Song Contest, but did have puppets. A different cut-out puppet appeared each week for over a year, so that the readers could make their very own Beano Puppet Show!

PUPPET ON A STRING Sandie Shaw

THE Beano AND Dandy TOP TEN FROM THE '60s

Korky the Cat had never been "Surfin' USA" like the Beach Boys, but in this 1967 tale, he wanted his chums to get rid of their "bushy blond hairdos" and change their image. (Coincidentally, on a 1967 Beach Boys LP there was a track titled "She's Goin' Bald" — was this where Korky got his idea from?!)

8

SURFIN' USA The Beach Boys

KORKY THE CAT
THEY USED TO BE ALL THE RAGE – BUT NOT NOW.
The BLEACH BOYS
LATER.
WHAT YOU NEED IS A NEW LOOK – A NEW HAIR STYLE AND A NEW NAME. COME WITH ME AND I'LL FIX YOU UP.
IT'S WORTH A TRY, FELLOWS!
AND SO AT KORKY'S BARBER SHOP.
SLEEP PILLS
NOW TAKE IT EASY. I'LL MAKE YOU ALL A CUP OF COFFEE BEFORE WE START.
HO-HO! THEY'RE ALL FAST ASLEEP! NOW FOR THE NEW HAIR STYLE.
ZZZ
ZZZZ
NNNN
LATER.
THERE YOU ARE, BOYS. AND I'VE THOUGHT UP A NEW NAME AS WELL.
The BAWLED BOYS
HOW ABOUT THAT THEN? AND THEY'VE EVEN LEARNED TO BAWL LOUDER!
25.2.67

PURPLE HAZE Jimi Hendrix Experience

The Jimi Hendrix Experience's hit single "Purple Haze" didn't quite reach the dizzy heights of the Number One Spot (peaking at Number Three in March '67, with a total of 14 weeks in the Charts) but could this song have been inspired by a story called "The Purple Cloud" which caused chaos and destruction in the cattle lands of the U.S.A. for 36 weeks in The Dandy back in 1961?

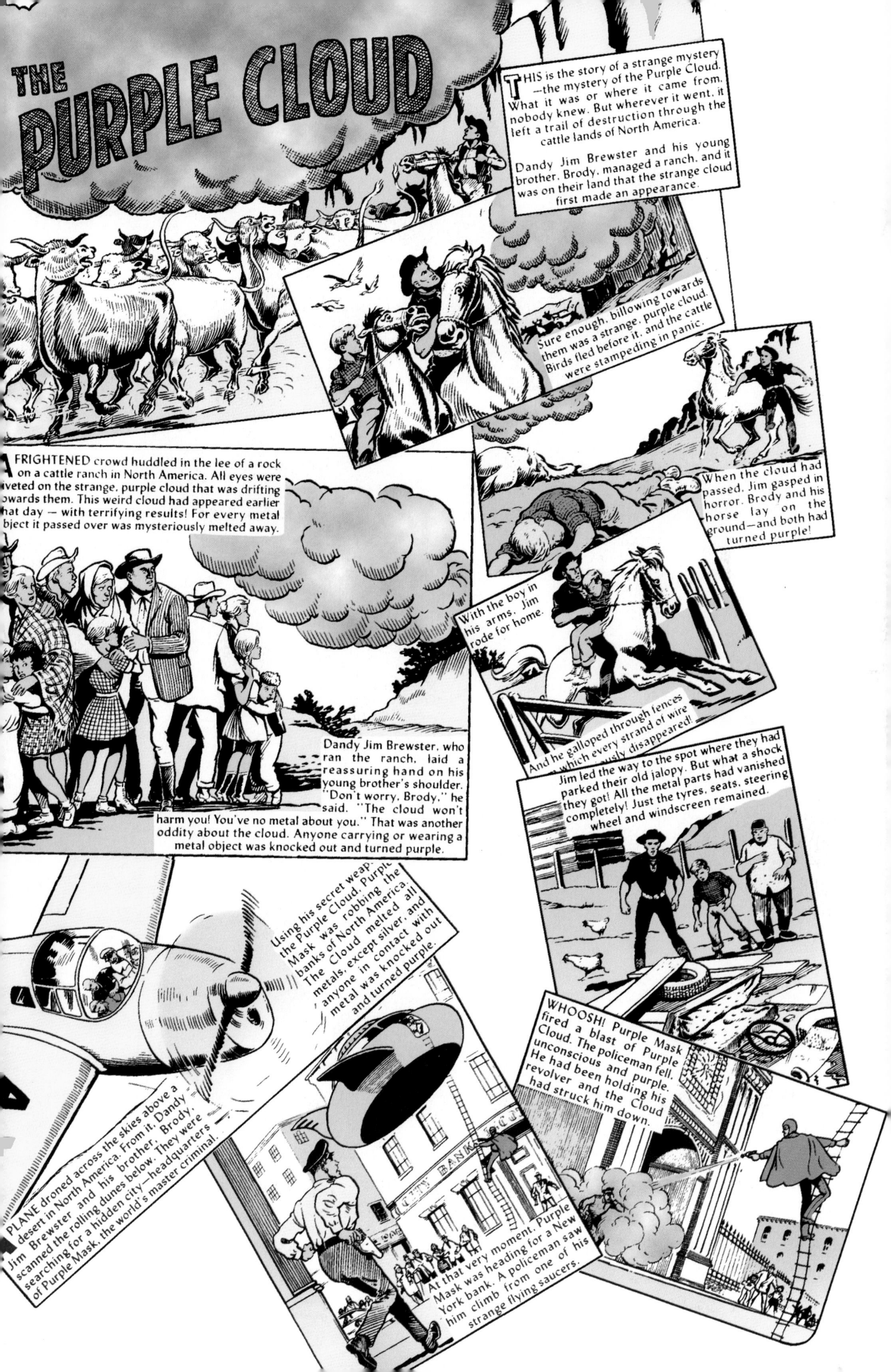
THE PURPLE CLOUD
THIS is the story of a strange mystery —the mystery of the Purple Cloud. What it was or where it came from, nobody knew. But wherever it went, it left a trail of destruction through the cattle lands of North America.
Dandy Jim Brewster and his young brother, Brody, managed a ranch, and it was on their land that the strange cloud first made an appearance.
Sure enough, billowing towards them was a strange, purple cloud. Birds fled before it, and the cattle were stampeding in panic.
When the cloud had passed, Jim gasped in horror. Brody and his horse lay on the ground—and both had turned purple!
A FRIGHTENED crowd huddled in the lee of a rock on a cattle ranch in North America. All eyes were fixed on the strange, purple cloud that was drifting towards them. This weird cloud had appeared earlier that day — with terrifying results! For every metal object it passed over was mysteriously melted away.
Dandy Jim Brewster, who ran the ranch, laid a reassuring hand on his young brother's shoulder. "Don't worry, Brody," he said. "The cloud won't harm you! You've no metal about you." That was another oddity about the cloud. Anyone carrying or wearing a metal object was knocked out and turned purple.
With the boy in his arms, Jim rode for home.
And he galloped through fences which every strand of wire mysteriously disappeared!
Jim led the way to the spot where they had parked their old jalopy. But what a shock they got! All the metal parts had vanished completely! Just the tyres, seats, steering wheel and windscreen remained.
Using his secret weapon, the Purple Cloud, Purple Mask was robbing the banks of North America. The Cloud melted all metals, except silver, and anyone in contact with metal was knocked out and turned purple.
A PLANE droned across the skies above a desert in North America. From it, Dandy Jim Brewster and his brother, Brody, scanned the rolling dunes below. They were searching for a hidden city—headquarters of Purple Mask, the world's master criminal.
At that very moment, Purple Mask was heading for a New York bank. A policeman saw him climb from one of his strange flying saucers.
WHOOSH! Purple Mask fired a blast of Purple Cloud. The policeman fell, unconscious and purple. He had been holding his revolver and the Cloud had struck him down.

BIG HEAD and THICK HEAD
WE'VE GOT ONLY A SHILLING BETWEEN US, SO WE'LL HAVE TO EARN SOME MONEY IF WE'RE TO GO TO THE PICTURES. LET'S SEE IF THERE ARE ANY JOBS GOING HERE.
KLUMP! KLUMP!
I'LL GIVE YOU FIVE SHILLINGS IF YOU CUT UP THESE LOGS. THERE'S A SAW IN THE SHED.
OKAY, LADY. WE'LL DO IT!
ZZZZZZ
STIFLED GROAN
I'LL GET THE SAW!
IT WILL TAKE A LOT OF HARD WORK TO SAW UP THAT LOT—AND I'M NOT DOING IT!
GOLLY! I CAN'T SEE A THING! THE SUN'S IN MY EYES!
WHY DON'T YOU TIE A HANDKERCHIEF OVER YOUR EYES, THEN?
GOOD IDEA.
PHEW! THIS IS—PUFF—HARD WORK. PANT!
PUFF! PANT! GASP! SO IT IS, THICK HEAD! CHUCKLE!
S-T-R-E-T-CH
WHILE HE'S BLINDFOLDING HIMSELF, I'LL BORROW THIS MAN'S BRACES.
WHISK
YOU MEDDLING LITTLE RUFFIAN! YOU'VE STRETCHED MY BRACES SO MUCH, I'D NEED TO BE NINE FEET TALL TO FIT THEM!
YIKES! I THINK I'D BETTER BEAT IT!
ONE HOUR LATER
PHEW! FINISHED AT LAST!
YES! I'M TIRED OUT! NOW IF YOU TAKE THE SAW BACK TO THE SHED, I'LL COLLECT OUR CASH!
THANKS VERY MUCH, LADY. OO-ER!
BELLOW!
SCREAM OF RAGE
FURIOUS HOWLS
LATER—
THAT'S SIX BOB WE HAVE NOW. WE CAN HAVE A SIXPENNY ICE EACH BEFORE THE SHOW.
CAFE
REGAL
NOW SHOWING
PAY HERE
THAT'S RIGHT. YOU PAY THE ICES AND I'LL PAY THE PICTURES. LET'S GO!
CLUB
BUT—
EEK! LOOK AT THE PRICES! THAT MEANS ONLY ONE OF US CAN GET IN!
SEATS AT 5/- ONLY
YES! IT'S A PITY YOU'LL MISS THE PICTURE, BUT I'VE BOUGHT MY TICKET. TA-TA, YOU MUG!
TAKE THAT FOR BUSTING MY BRACES! AND DON'T COME BACK HERE AGAIN!
BAM!
COME TO ME, TICKET!
HO-HO! BIG HEAD'S SEEING STARS NOW—BUT THEY'RE NOT FILM STARS!
OOH
27.5.67
KERRUMP!

THE Beano AND Dandy TOP TEN FROM THE '60s

The Rolf Harris hit "Two Little Boys" was the final chart-topper of the '60s. In the song, "each had a wooden horse", but in this Big Head and Thick Head story from 1967, each had a wooden SAW-horse!

10 TWO LITTLE BOYS Rolf Harris

Note for really keen comic fans — the caricatures of the Beatles used on these pages are taken from a Dandy page: My Home Town (Liverpool) issue dated 1.2.64.

The 'Fab Four', as The Beatles were called, influenced many things during the '60's — including The Dandy! On these pages are a 'Fab Three' tales which prove that even long-standing favourites like Dennis the Menace and Korky the Cat experienced the Beatles phenomenon.
KORKY'S BARBER SHOP
KORKY THE CAT
13.6.64
KORKY THE GLASS HAIRDRESSER
THIS SHOULD BRING IN THE CUSTOMERS.
GET A FABULOUS AMERICAN CREW-CUT HERE!
THIS WAY, SIR— YOU'RE FIRST.
CLICK
NOW WATCH MY QUICK WAY OF TURNING A BEATLE GROWTH INTO A CREW-CUT!
YOW!
QUICKEST HAIRCUT I'VE EVER HAD!
SNIP SNIP
AT PROFESSOR PLUNK'S ACADEMY OF MUSIC—
THAT'S LOVELY, WALTER. LET DENNIS TRY NOW.
SWEET MUSIC
HUH! THAT'S OLD-FASHIONED STUFF!
I'M A MEH-NACE! YEAH! YEAH! YEAH!
TWANG!
OH, HOW HORRIBLE!
George
GRR!
THIS IS NO USE TO ME—YOU CAN HAVE IT BACK!
HERE'S THE CORNET, NASTY BOY.
BUT WHERE'S THE ICE-CREAM, LONG-NOSE?
JAM!
BACK AT THE HOUSE—
YOUR SON'S BEEN EXPELLED FROM MY ACADEMY. PLEASE ACCEPT THIS BOOK AND THESE DRUMSTICKS. I THINK YOU'LL HAVE A USE FOR THEM.
I WILL INDEED!
LEARN HOW TO PLAY THE DRUMS
BUT DAD HASN'T GOT A DRUM!
OH, NO?—
I THINK I MUST BE THE MUSICAL ONE OF THE FAMILY AFTER ALL!
Drum Music BOOM! THUMP BOOM BAM
BAM!
THUMP!
BOOM!
22.2.64
Ringo

5.9.64

The Beatles even influenced a Corporal Clott story from 1964.

I KNOW THE BARBER HAS BEEN OFF DUTY A LONG TIME, BUT I'M NOT GOING TO HAVE YOU ALL LOOKING LIKE BEATLES! CORPORAL CLOTT HERE HAS HIS SCISSORS SHARPENED. REPORT TO HIS BARBER SHOP IMMEDIATELY!

OOGH! THE PLACE IS FULL OF SMOKE!
THAT'S RIGHT! FREE SMOKE!

CAUGHT THEM IN MY TRAP! SHORT BACK AND SIDES, LADS?
GOR! MY BEATLE LOOK RUINED!

AND ROUND THE CORNER CLOTT HAS ARRANGED A TRAP FOR THEM!
TRIP!

SHOVE! PUSH! AND RUN!
THEIR HEADS ARE STUCK IN THE RAILINGS. NOW TO GIVE THEM A QUICK TRIM!

JUMPING CATS!
THEY COULDN'T GET THEIR HEADS OUT, SO LOOK WHAT THEY'VE DONE INSTEAD!

WELL, THAT RAILING TRICK WON'T WORK A SECOND TIME, SO ON TO TRICK NUMBER THREE– CLOTT'S SPECIAL HAIR-CREAM TRICK!

THERE YOU ARE, ALEC! BEST HAIR CREAM BARGAIN EVER OFFERED. BRING THE JAR BACK FOR A REFILL AT HALF-PRICE!
1d A JAR
SMASHING SMELL THIS HAIR-CREAM'S GOT!

GOR! OUR HATS HAVE STUCK TO OU HAIR! THERE WAS GLUE IN THAT HAIR CREAM!

HUH! NOBODY'S TURNED UP! HAVE TO DO SOMETHING ABOUT IT!
THIS NOTICE SHOULD FETCH THEM IN!
FREE SMOKES Q HERE
BARBER
FREE FAGS! BOY, OH, BOY!
FIRST FOUR!
'60S
THAT'S US! HERE WE COME!
I CAN'T PLAY THAT TRICK AGAIN, SO I'LL USE THIS LION SKIN FOR MY NEXT HAIR-RAISING DODGE!
ROAR!
RUN!
OH, MOTHER! A LION LOOSE IN THE CAMP!
HO-HO! I'M GOING TO CHASE THEM ROUND THE CORNER!
HELP!
BUT–
HO-HO! THEY'RE TRAPPED! THE RAILINGS HAVE GOT WEDGED!
HOW DO YOU LIKE YOURS DONE, CLAUDE? IS THAT SHORT ENOUGH?
I'D RATHER HAVE BEEN A LION'S DINNER!
THERE'S ONLY ONE WAY TO GET YOUR HATS OFF–AND THAT IS TO CUT THEM OFF! HOW'S THAT, PRIVATE PERKINS?
LATER.
COME HERE, CLOTT! YOU'VE HAD YOUR FUN! NOW WE'LL HAVE OURS!
HO-HO! WE'VE MADE A SPECIAL WIG FOR CLOTT AND STUCK IT ON WITH HIS OWN HAIR CREAM!
THAT'LL TAKE SOME SHIFTING! IT'S A PERMANENT WAVE!

Minnie THE Minx
MINNIE, YOUR HAIR'S A MESS...
...I'M GOING TO GIVE YOU A PERM— COME BACK!
I LIKE MY HAIR THE WAY IT IS!
LATER, STILL—
WHERE'S MIN?
HAVING A BATH, I THINK—I HEARD THE WATER RUNNING.
LATER—
THERE! WHAT DO YOU THINK OF IT?
I THINK IT'S...
...TERRIBLE!
SO—
TUM-TEE-TUM! JUST GIVING MYSELF ANOTHER PERM, READERS.
HOME PERM
YAHOO! I KNOW!
HOW CAN I GET RID OF THESE CURLS?
Never mind the Beatles' hair styles — Do you think Minnie The Minx has always had the same hairstyle? Think again! Just look at Min's expressions in this 1967 Beano "hairy tale" — they'll make your hair curl!

DAD!
SO—
ER—LET'S TALK THIS OVER—NO NEED TO BE HASTY...
BUT—
THERE'S NOTHING TO TALK OVER. YOU'RE GETTING A PERM!
OOO!
THEN—
SHE'S UP TO SOMETHING—SHE NEVER HAS A BATH WITHOUT SOMEBODY TELLING HER TO!
SO! TRYING TO SOAK OUT YOUR PERM, EH?
HEH! HEH! IT'S A BIT OF LUCK THAT THE CURLS DON'T COME OUT IN WATER, ISN'T IT?
A BIT OF BAD LUCK, YOU MEAN!
WHIRR!
LATER—
YOO-HOO, MUM—HOW DO YOU LIKE MY NEW HAIRSTYLE?
FAINT
HERE—GO TO THE HAIRDRESSER'S AND HAVE IT DONE PROPERLY.
THANKS, DAD!
SO—
HUH! WE MIGHT HAVE GUESSED!
THIS IS MORE LIKE IT, EH, READERS?
'60s

2.12.67

Today, hovercraft can be seen mainly in common use as high-speed ferry vehicles, but in the '60s they were seen as something out of science-fiction

SEND FOR the HOVERTANK

The Beano's "Hovertank" was set to save the world for roughly seven months, back in 1969.

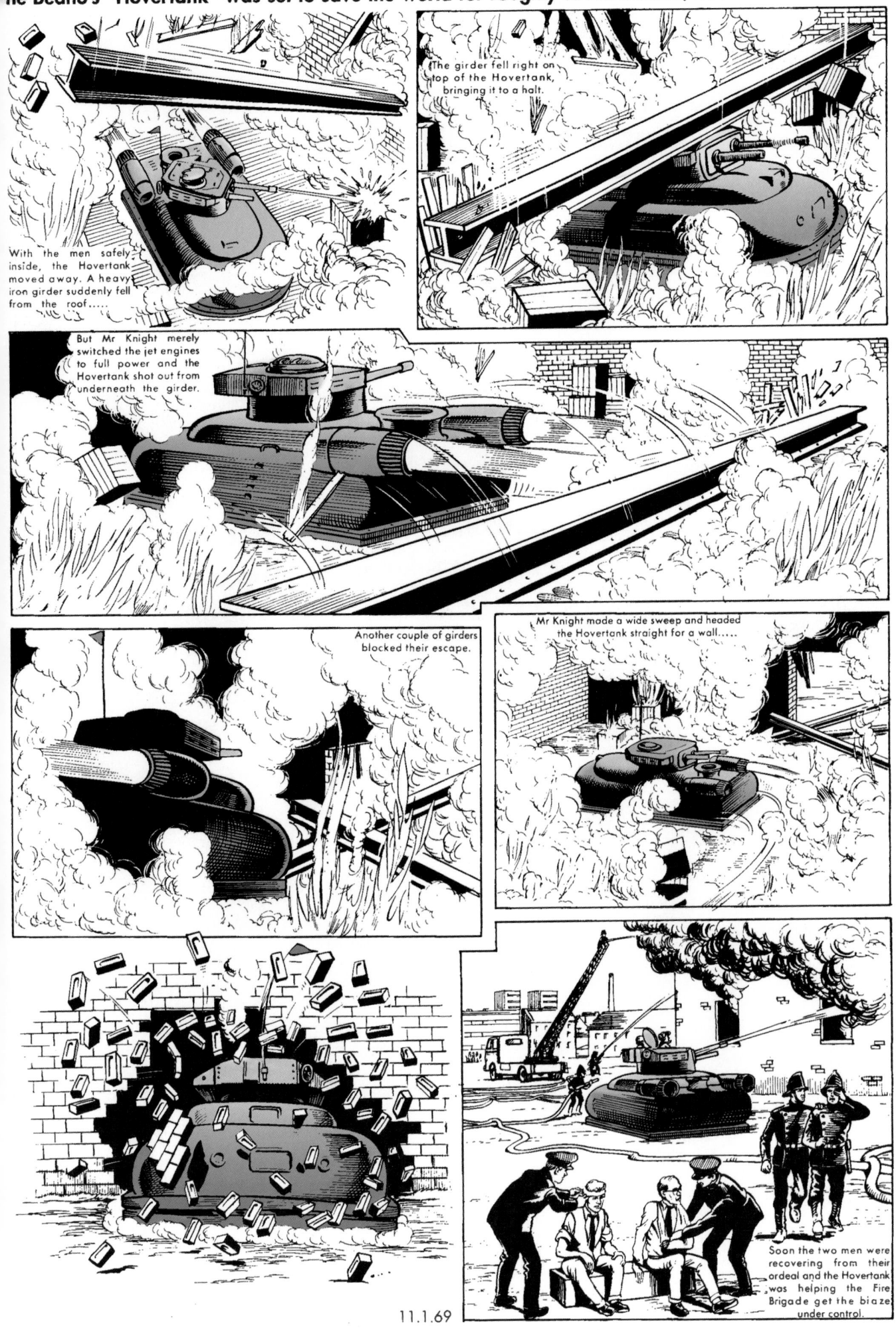

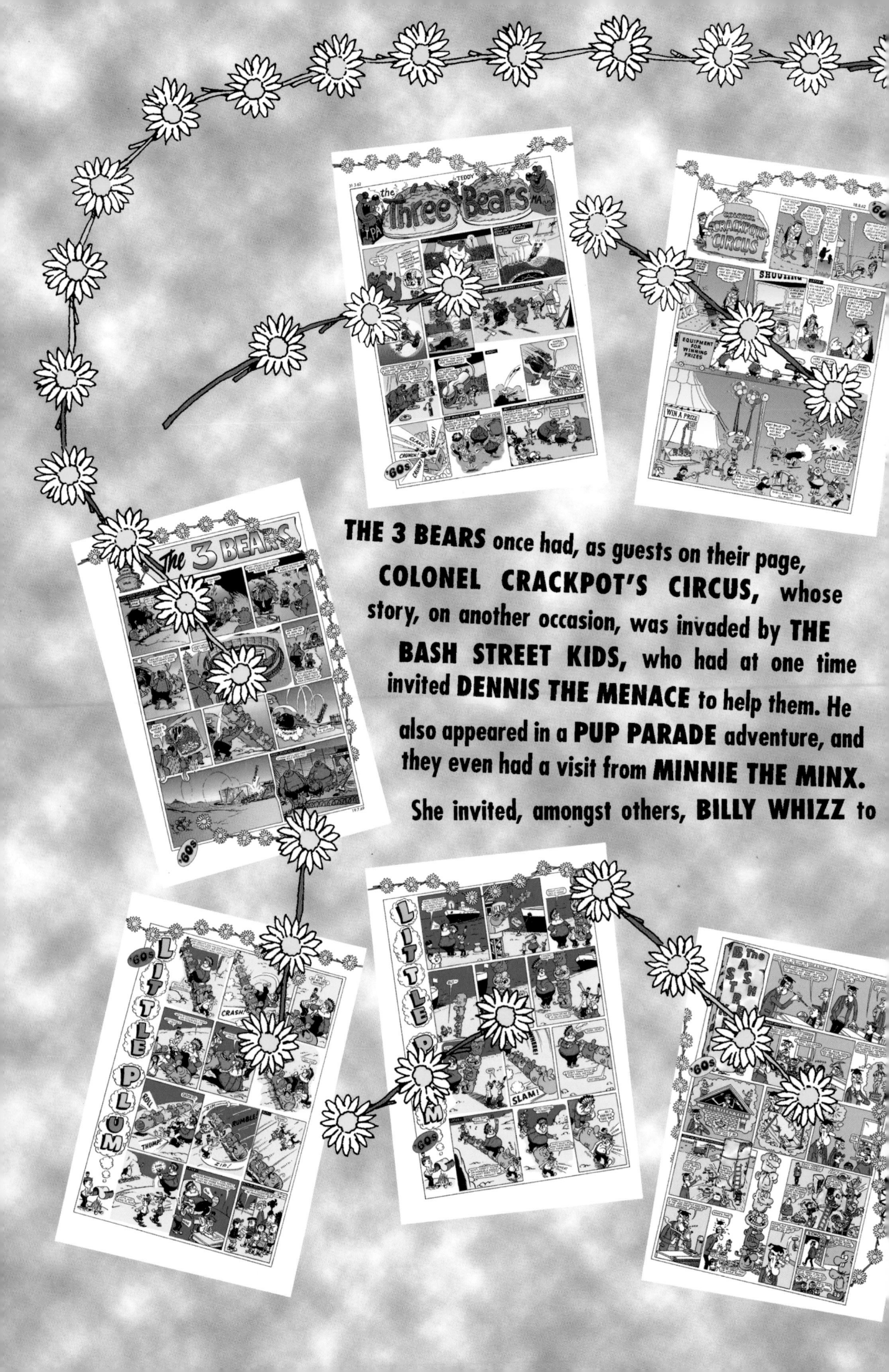

THE 3 BEARS once had, as guests on their page, **COLONEL CRACKPOT'S CIRCUS,** whose story, on another occasion, was invaded by **THE BASH STREET KIDS,** who had at one time invited **DENNIS THE MENACE** to help them. He also appeared in a **PUP PARADE** adventure, and they even had a visit from **MINNIE THE MINX.** She invited, amongst others, **BILLY WHIZZ** to

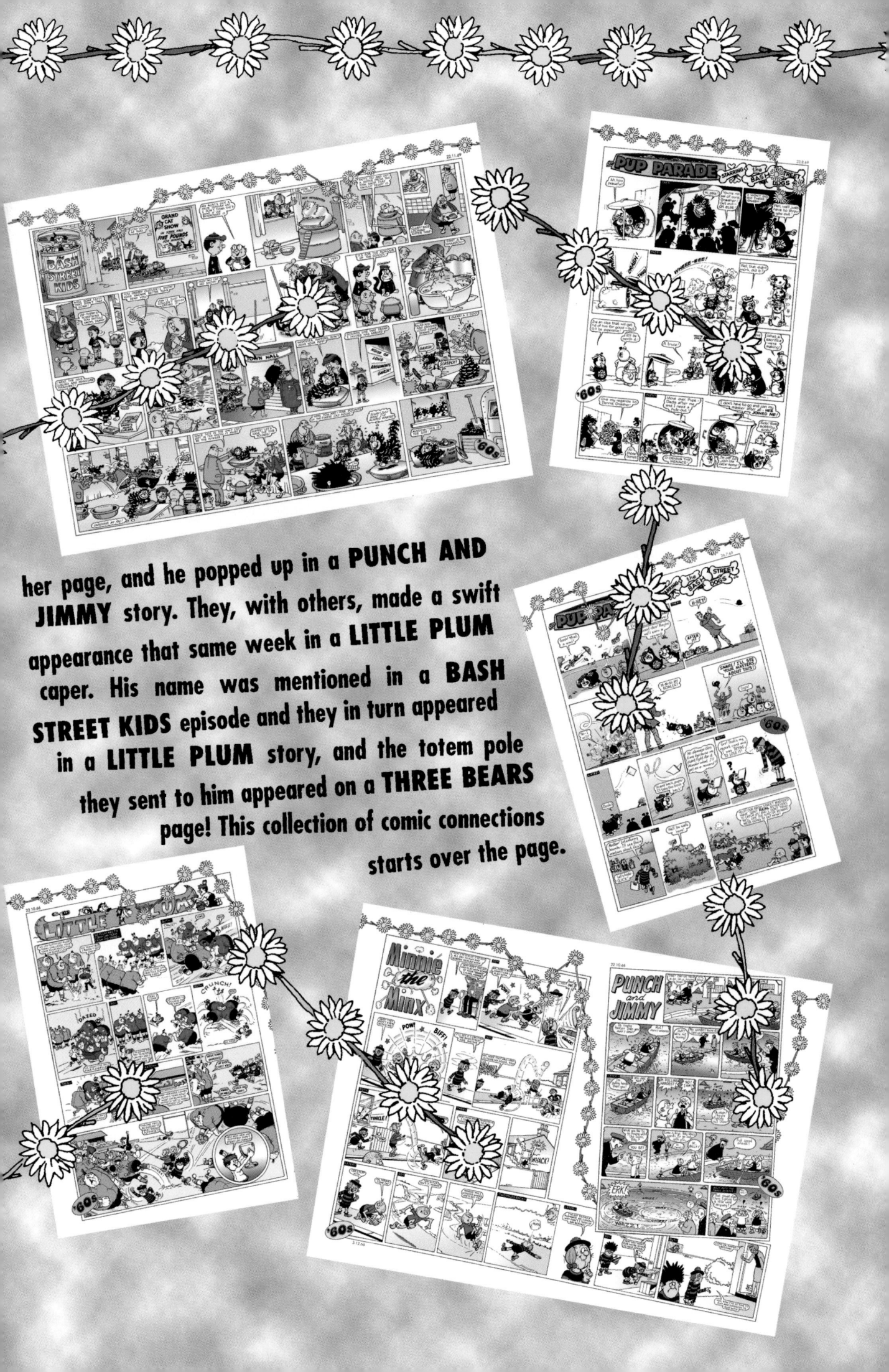

her page, and he popped up in a **PUNCH AND JIMMY** story. They, with others, made a swift appearance that same week in a **LITTLE PLUM** caper. His name was mentioned in a **BASH STREET KIDS** episode and they in turn appeared in a **LITTLE PLUM** story, and the totem pole they sent to him appeared on a **THREE BEARS** page! This collection of comic connections starts over the page.

31.3.62

the Three Bears
TEDDY
PA
MA
THAT'S THE JOB FOR US.
COLONEL CRACKPOT'S CIRCUS WANTED PERFORMING BEARS THREE SQUARE MEALS PER DAY
SO—
PRESENTING—THE ONLY "BEAR"-BACK RIDER IN THE WORLD.
NEXT—THE DARING YOUNG BEAR ON THE FLYING TRAPEZE.
ALLEZ-OOP!
NEVER BE WITHOUT A "BEANO"
IT'S EASY, READERS. I USE MAGNETS AND A METAL TRAPEZE BAR.
THEN AN UNUSUAL TRAMPOLINE ACT—
BEANO
BOING!
BOING!
DINNER TIME—AND THE BEARS LEAD THE RUSH—
SLURP!
BONG!
AGH! THE COLONEL'S IDEA OF A SQUARE MEAL IS ONE BEEF CUBE.
YOU BEARS ARE TO BE FIRED FROM A CANNON AT THE AFTERNOON SHOW!
FOLKS! YOU WILL NOW SEE THREE HAIRY CANNONBALLS!
HEH! HEH! I'LL JUST MAKE A SLIGHT ADJUSTMENT TO THE AIMING DEVICE!
AND—
BOOM!
YIPPEE! RIGHT ON TARGET!
FOOD CARAVAN
FOOD STORE
CLANG!
CRASH!
CRUNCH!
CRUMP!
'60s
TEN MINUTES LATER—
WAH! THEY'VE GUZZLED A MONTH'S SUPPLY OF GRUB AT ONE SITTING!
FOOD STORE
BELCH!
BUT THE COLONEL FINDS THAT HE NOW HAS A NEW ACT.
LADIES AND GENTLEMEN! PRESENTING — THE FATTEST GOLDILOCKS AND THE FATTEST THREE BEARS IN THE WORLD.
WHO'S BEEN EATIN' OUR PORRIDGE?

18.8.62
'60s
COLONEL CRACKPOT'S CIRCUS
YOUR POCKET MONEY? ALL RIGHT— HERE IT IS.
THE OLD SKINFLINT GRUDGES EVERY HALFPENNY OF THAT TWO SHILLINGS HE GIVES ME EACH WEEK.
WHY DON'T YOU SPEND YOUR MONEY AT THE FUN FAIR STALLS, CYRIL? YOU MIGHT WIN SOME SUPER PRIZES!
HEH! HEH! I'VE FIXED IT SO THAT EVEN A CIRCUS STRONG-MAN COULDN'T RING THE BELL!
A PRIZE IF YOU RING THE BELL
PUT THE BALL IN THE PAIL AND WIN A PRIZE
3 BALLS for 6d
HEH! HEH! THE PAILS HAVE GOT SPECIAL SPRINGY BOTTOMS! HO! HO!
BONK!
BOING!
SHOOTING
A PRIZE FOR EVERY BALL YOU HIT
CRACK!
HEH! HEH! THE RIFLE BARRELS ARE SLIGHTLY TWISTED!
LATER—
YOU HAVEN'T WON A SINGLE PRIZE, CYRIL—AND I'VE GOT YOUR TWO SHILLINGS BACK! HEH! HEH!
DO YOU MIND IF I BRING SOME LITTLE FRIENDS TO HAVE A GO AT THE STALLS, UNC?
OF COURSE NOT, M'BOY—AS LONG AS YOUR LITTLE FRIENDS HAVE LOTS OF LITTLE SIXPENCES!
LATER
EQUIPMENT FOR WINNING PRIZES
HIYA, CYRIL!
HERE COME MY LITTLE FRIENDS, UNC!
GOSH! THE BASH STREET KIDS!
WIN A PRIZE
PUT THE BALL IN THE PAIL AND WIN A PRIZE
3 BALLS for 6d
PLUP!
LIFT ME AND WIN A PRIZE
STALLS
EIGHT BALLS WITH ONE SHOT! NOT BAD SHOOTIN'!
SHOOT
DID YOUR UNCLE TELL YOU WHERE HE KEPT THE PRIZES BEFORE HE FAINTED?
HA! HA! HA!
ONE MORE PAILFUL AND WE'LL HAVE WON TWO THOUSAND PRIZES!
THIS'LL RING THE BELL ALL RIGHT!

The BASH STREET KIDS
COO! LOOK AT THAT!
GRAND CAT SHOW
IN TOWN HALL
FIVE POUNDS FOR WINNER!
MY AUNT'S GOT A PRIZE PERSIAN CAT. I DON'T THINK SHE'D MIND IF WE BORROWED IT.
WELL DONE, FATTY! THAT DIDN'T TAKE LONG!
ER-THERE'S SOMETHING YOU SHOULD KNOW, DANNY!
YOU GREEDY GUZZLER! I MIGHT HAVE KNOWN BETTER THAN SEND YOU!
ERK! I JUST COULDN'T RESIST EATING IT!
HUH! NO CAT-NO SHOW!
-NEXT, THE HAIR CURLING AND MANICURE TREATMENT-
MANICURE SET
DANNY'S MUM'S CURLERS
-JUST A HINT OF PERFUME!
DANNY'S MUM'S PERFUME
SO-
TOWN
CAT SHOW TODAY
GNASHER'S MY PAL!
SINCE THIS IS THE ONLY CAT LEFT IN THE SHOW, IT MUST BE THE WINNER!
YIPPEE! LET'S HAVE THE FIVE POUNDS!

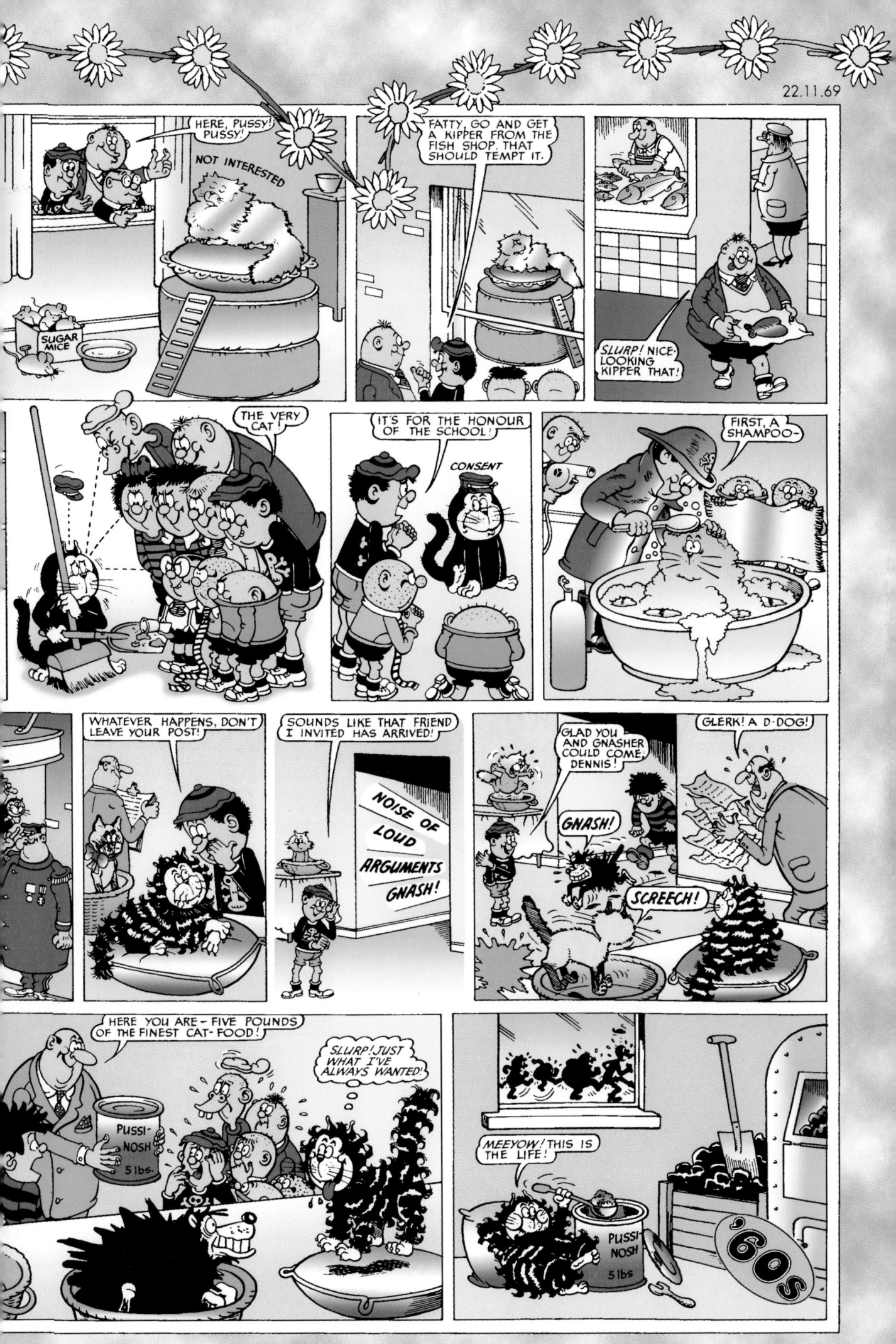
22.11.69
HERE, PUSSY! PUSSY!
NOT INTERESTED
SUGAR MICE
FATTY, GO AND GET A KIPPER FROM THE FISH SHOP. THAT SHOULD TEMPT IT.
SLURP! NICE-LOOKING KIPPER THAT!
THE VERY CAT!
IT'S FOR THE HONOUR OF THE SCHOOL!
CONSENT
FIRST, A SHAMPOO-
WHATEVER HAPPENS, DON'T LEAVE YOUR POST!
SOUNDS LIKE THAT FRIEND I INVITED HAS ARRIVED!
NOISE OF LOUD ARGUMENTS GNASH!
GLAD YOU AND GNASHER COULD COME, DENNIS!
GLERK! A D-DOG!
GNASH!
SCREECH!
HERE YOU ARE - FIVE POUNDS OF THE FINEST CAT-FOOD!
SLURP! JUST WHAT I'VE ALWAYS WANTED!
PUSSI-NOSH 5 lbs.
MEEYOW! THIS IS THE LIFE!
PUSSI NOSH 5 lbs
'60s

23.8.69
PUP PARADE
STARRING the BASH STREET DOGS
Ah, how peaceful!
THEN-
Hi, pals!
You're no pal of ours, Gnasher! Get out – OR ELSE!
I WON'T GO, SO THERE! GNASH!
Well, we'll just have to throw you out!
SO-
THUMP!
CRASH!
THUD!
THEN-
WHEEE-EEE!
CRUMP!
Well, that didn't work, did it?
I've an idea that will get rid of him for good – but it'll be expensive!
It'll be worth it!
SO-
WHITE FLAG (ONLY IT GOT DIRTY?)
A truce!
Gnash!
Mr Gnasher, sir, we'll give you all our bones if you go back and join your master and stop bothering us!
What a sacrifice we're making!
OK!
'60s
Give my regards to Dennis, Gnasher!
All those bones!
THEN-
Move over, Pups – Dad's after me, and I need a hide-out!
D-DENNIS THE MENACE!
I don't have to go and join my master after all – HE'S JOINED ME!
Sob! Sob! sobbity, sob!
WAH!
I'm off to join the cats' home!

26.7.69
PUPPARADE
STARRING the BASH STREET DOGS
Gosh! What a wind!
Let's be retrievers - we can take back lost hats and things to their owners!
Good idea! Maybe we'll earn a reward!
THEN-
H-HEY!
AFTER IT!
I'll get it!
THUD!
No - I will!
SO-
M-M-M-MY BOWLER!
SNARL! I'LL SEE YOUR MASTERS ABOUT THIS!
Oops!
'60s
LATER-
Oooh!
Stand back, pups! I'll take this book back!
No damage this time because we didn't fight for it. Wonder what I'll get as a reward?
BUT-
Grr! That's my report card and I was TRYING TO LOSE IT!
?
Mutter! Interfering hounds - I'll see their masters about this!
Let's hide - QUICK!
SO-
We'll be safe here!
BUT-
YELP! OUR BASH STREET MASTERS HAVE SENT REAL RETRIEVERS TO CATCH US! AND I DON'T THINK WE'LL LIKE THE KIND OF REWARD WE'RE GOING TO GET NOW!

Minnie the Minx
HUH! I'M FED UP! I'VE GOT ALL DAY TO PLAY AND NOBODY TO PLAY WITH!
WHY DON'T YOU GO AND PLAY WITH SOME OF YOUR "BEANO" CHUMS, MINNIE?
SO—
AH, PUNCH AND JIMMY! CAN I PLAY WITH...
POW!
...YOU?
OW!
CRACK!
GASP! THEY DIDN'T EVEN NOTICE ME!
POW!
BIFF!
BOP!
I'LL SEE IF I CAN FIND THE BASH STREET KIDS INSTEAD.
SO—
AH, HERE THEY ARE—AND OUTSIDE MY HOUSE, TOO!
BUT—
TINKLE!
WOW!
GOSH! YOU'VE DONE IT NOW! LET'S GO, KIDS!
THEN—
GRR! HOW MANY TIMES HAVE I TOLD YOU NOT TO PLAY FOOTBALL IN THE STREET?
B—BUT...
ZIP!
WHACK!
HOWL!
WHACK!
LATER—
CAN I PLAY WITH...
OK, MINNIE. COME ON!
SO—
THIS IS FUN, ISN'T IT, MINNIE?
ZIP!
MINNIE! HM! I WONDER WHERE SHE'S GOT TO?
TWO MILES BACK—
PUFF!
'60s
3.12.66

22.10.66
PUNCH and JIMMY
Dad! Can we have a go on a towing boat?
O.K, boys.
BOATS FOR HIRE
HIRE
I'm towing faster than you! PUFF! GASP!
Rot! PUFF! WHEEZE!
Puff! We're not moving!
No wonder! You're still tied up!
Away you go now, boys.
BLUSH
BLUSH
LATER–
I'm pulling harder than you!
YOU ARE NOT!
I'M PULLING HARDEST!
NO! I AM!
Hmm! It's Billy Whizz!
BASH!
BOOF!
Oh, dear! They're fighting out there!
SCREECH!
Would you like to go rowing with the twins, Billy?
YOU BET!
Come in, boys. Billy Whizz wants to go out with you.
HI, TWINS!
HI, BILLY!
Full speed ahead!
'60s
ERK!
WHIZZ!
WHIZZ!
WHIZZ!
WHIZZ!
?
?
BILLY PUTS THE TWINS ASHORE–
That should stop them fighting for a little while anyway!
HEE! HEE!
DIZZY
DIZZY
LATER–
I'VE GOT TO FIND A PLAYMATE. AH, I KNOW! WHY DIDN'T I THINK OF HIM BEFORE?
SO–
HEH! HEH! WHAT FUN WE'RE GOING TO HAVE, DENNIS!
BUT–
COME ON, MINNIE– BEDTIME!
HUH! NOW I'VE NO TIME TO PLAY AND SOMEBODY TO PLAY WITH!

22.10.66

LITTLE PLUM
WE-UM PUTTYFOOT RUGBY TEAM—CHALLENGE YOUR TEAM TO UM MATCH FOR UM SUPER CUP.
MY TEAM? BUT I HAVEN'T GOT ONE!
WHEEE!
ZIP!
SO PLUM HAS TO FORM UM TEAM FROM HIS TRIBE—
WE'LL HAVE UM PRACTICE SCRUM FIRST.
BUT—
CRACK!
YOWL!
HELP!
WHEEE!
ZIP!
WHIZZ!
DAZED
OH, GOSH! I'VE ONLY FOUR PLAYERS LEFT!
SO—
I'M GOING TO TRY TO SCORE UM TRY AND I WANT YOU TO STOP ME.
HERE I COME!
GET READY TO POUNCE ON HIM!
BUT—
CRUNCH!
EEK!
OH, DEAR!
THEN—
GOSH! WHERE CAN I GET UM TEAM NOW?
ON UM DAY OF UM MATCH—
HAR! HAR!HERE COMES PLUM'S TEAM NOW! WHAT UM BUNCH OF MIDGETS! WE'LL MASH THEM UP!
BUT—
ARGH! DENNIS UM MENACE!
UM BASH STREET KIDS!
MINNIE UM MINX!
PUNCH AND JIMMY!
SO—
THIS ONE TRY'LL BE ENOUGH TO BEAT THOSE PUTTYFEET!
WHEEE!
BOUNCE
HEH! HEH! HEH! UM PUTTYFEET DIDN'T STAND UM CHANCE!
'60S

28.6.69
The BASH STREET KIDS
'60s
HOW WOULD YOU LIKE TO HAVE A NICE ART LESSON, DOING PAINTING?
NOT LIKELY! REMEMBER WHAT HAPPENED LAST TIME - WE ENDED UP HAVING TO REDECORATE THE CLASSROOM!
ALL RIGHT, THEN. HOW WOULD YOU LIKE TO DO SOME SCULPTURE?
SCULPTURE? SUPER!
I'LL GO AND SHARPEN MY CARVING CHISEL!
I'D HAVE THOUGHT YOU'D BE USING YOUR TEETH! I'M CARVING MY LOLLY!
NEXT MORNING -
GOOD MORNING, CHILDREN! I'VE ORDERED THE BLOCK OF STONE, AND IT WILL BE DELIVERED TODAY.
I THINK I'LL CARVE YOU, TOOTS!
CARVE POOR TOOTS? YOU REALLY OUGHT TO USE STONE!
P·R·O·U·D
NOW, WHAT SORT OF THING WILL THEY CARVE, I WONDER? PERHAPS A MONUMENT TO THEIR BELOVED TEACHER?
TEACHER
MCLLIIICVVIII
OR COULD IT BE LIKE THIS?
OR PERHAPS...?
HERE'S THE STONE!
OUT IN THE PLAYGROUND -
BASH STREET SCHOOL
THERE YOU ARE, PUPILS - IT'S ALL YOURS!
I SHALL TAKE STEPS TO CARVE THIS STONE!
SUCH INTEREST! SUCH INTEREST!
CHIP THE STONE, NOT THE LADDER, YOU ASS!
BASH!
I NEVER THOUGHT I'D SEE SO MANY CHIPS WITHOUT BEING ABLE TO EAT THEM!
BASH!
I THINK I'LL GO OUT AND SEE IF THE KIDS HAVE FINISHED THEIR CARVING.
LICK
PAINTART
WHAT'S THAT?
IT'S A TOTEM POLE!
WE'RE GREAT FANS OF LITTLE PLUM!
MAYBE, BUT WE CAN'T HAVE THAT HERE! GET RID OF IT!
SCHOOL
I'LL HAVE TO ORDER SOME MORE STONE.
LET'S SEND IT ON TO PLUM, THEN IT WON'T BE WASTED.
HE'LL HAVE IT BY NEXT WEEK.

LITTLE PLUM
HERE COMES UM TOTEM POLE THAT UM BASH STREET KIDS MADE FOR US LAST WEEK!
JOY
TO PLUM
ADMIRATION
RIGHT—LET'S GET IT HOME.
BUT—
—HOW?
I KNOW—CARRY IT!
BUT HOW DO WE GET IT ON ITS SIDE?
EASY!
HUH?
WHEEE!
SLAM!
SCRATCH
OOOH, DEAR!
I DIDN'T THINK MUCH OF THAT IDEA, DID YOU, PIMPLE?
NOT REALLY!
'60s
LATER—
TOTE THAT BARGE...
GLEAM
QUIET, CHIEFY! YOU'RE UM HORRIBLE SINGER! WH-WHAT DOES "TOTE" MEAN, ANYWAY?
"TOTE" MEANS "CARRY".
THAT MUST BE HOW THESE POLES GOT THEIR NAME...
SWEAT
... ALL I EVER DO IS TOTE 'EM!
STEAM
SWEAT

'60s
LITTLE PLUM
WHY AREN'T YOU HELPING TO CARRY UM TOTEM POLE WE GOT FROM UM BASH STREET KIDS LAST WEEK?
BECAUSE I'M SUPERVISING!
EEK!
CRASH!
GRR!
CRASH!
YOU ARE NOT SUPER ANYTHING!
WOULD YOU KINDLY SHIFT UM TOTEM POLE?
WHY SHOULD WE?
BECAUSE IT'S ON MY FOOT!
OOOH!
SO—
EEK! EEK!
CATCH IT!
ROLL
THUMP!
ZIP!
RUMBLE!
ZIP!
BUT—
GROAN!
SORE
LET'S JUST LEAVE IT, HUH?
SORE
LATER—
"DEAR BASH STREET KIDS, DON'T SEND US ANY MORE TOTEM POLES—THEY'RE TOO DANGEROUS!"
PAIN
SORE
ACHE
ACHE
BACK IN BASH STREET—
HOW CAN A TOTEM POLE BE DANGEROUS?

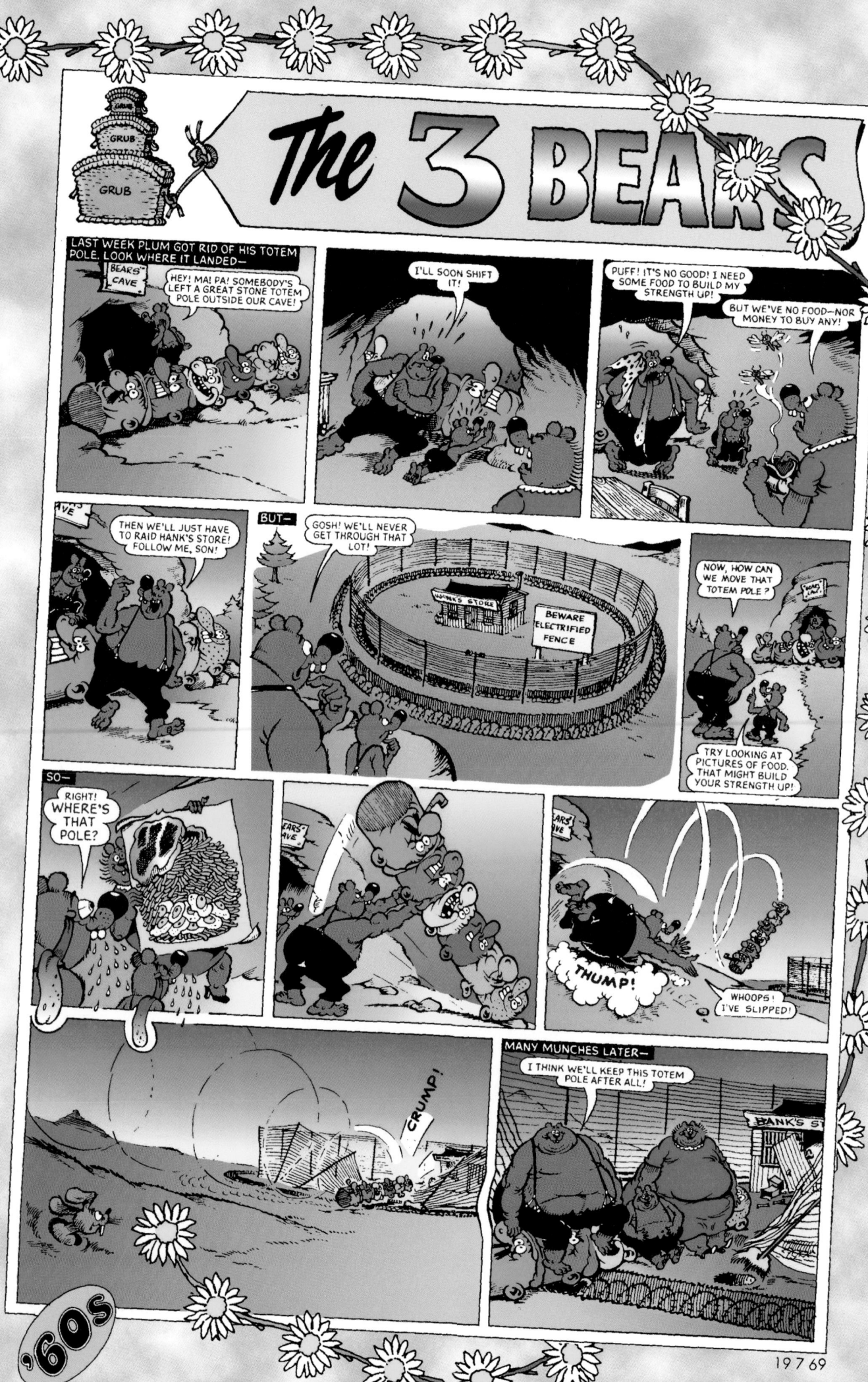
GRUB
GRUB
The 3 BEARS
LAST WEEK PLUM GOT RID OF HIS TOTEM POLE. LOOK WHERE IT LANDED—
BEARS' CAVE
HEY! MA! PA! SOMEBODY'S LEFT A GREAT STONE TOTEM POLE OUTSIDE OUR CAVE!
I'LL SOON SHIFT IT!
PUFF! IT'S NO GOOD! I NEED SOME FOOD TO BUILD MY STRENGTH UP!
BUT WE'VE NO FOOD—NOR MONEY TO BUY ANY!
THEN WE'LL JUST HAVE TO RAID HANK'S STORE! FOLLOW ME, SON!
BUT—
GOSH! WE'LL NEVER GET THROUGH THAT LOT!
HANK'S STORE
BEWARE ELECTRIFIED FENCE
NOW, HOW CAN WE MOVE THAT TOTEM POLE?
TRY LOOKING AT PICTURES OF FOOD. THAT MIGHT BUILD YOUR STRENGTH UP!
SO—
RIGHT! WHERE'S THAT POLE?
THUMP!
WHOOPS! I'VE SLIPPED!
CRUMP!
MANY MUNCHES LATER—
I THINK WE'LL KEEP THIS TOTEM POLE AFTER ALL!
'60s
1976 9

Want to know about fashion in the Sixties? Who better to show you than someone who's had a fur coat since 1937 . . . The Dandy's former front-page fun-pal —

To begin this section of '60s fashion — here's Jonah with something that's gone OUT of fashion!

'60s
24.3.62
WE NO SAILSKI IN CASE JONAHSKI SINKS USKI!
HONOULABLE JAPANESE SAILORS RATHER SUFFER HOLLIBLE JAPANESE TORTURE THAN GO TO SEA WITH JONAH ALOUND!
SO, AS THE OCEANS BECOME EMPTY OF SHIPPING —
GONE QUIET, HASN'T IT, HERBERT?
FOR HE'S A JOLLY GOOD FELLOW!
HOORAY!
SO, TWO DAYS LATER, IN ANSWER TO AN ADVERTISEMENT IN THE "NAUTICAL NEWS," JONAH MEETS BLUNT AND SIMPKINS ON THE SHORES OF LOCH THINGMY IN BONNIE SCOTLAND.
AHEM! – IN VIEW OF YOUR OUTSTANDING KNOWLEDGE OF SHIPS, I WANT YOU TO TAKE CHARGE OF THE LOCH THINGMY FERRY!
COR!
ROUND THE HEADLAND —
AWLK!
SOME RAT'S BUILT A BRIDGE! NO WONDER I GOT NO PASSENGERS!

This Lord Snooty story highlighted the fashions during the clothing . . . er . . . closing years of the decade.

Greenwich Village, New York, was the fashionable place to be, forty years ago. Unfortunately, Little Plum and Chiefy lived in Smellyfeet Village . . .
WEST 14th STREET
EAST 14th ST.
GREENWICH AVE.
8th AVE.
7th AVE. SOUTH
BLEECKER ST.
HUDSON
WEST STREET
6th AVE.
5th AVE.
WASHINGTON SQUARE PARK
BROADWAY
WEST HOUSTON STREET
WEST HOUSTON STREET
I'VE BOUGHT UM SHOP. YOU WON'T RECOGNISE IT WHEN I'VE DECORATED IT.
LATER-
PLUM'S BOUTIQUE
ALL UM LATEST FASHIONS
THERE! ISN'T IT UM BEAUTY NOW?
SO-
I WANT UM PAIR OF HIPSTER TROUGERS, SHOES AND UM SIVEATER, PLEASE, PLUM.
OK, CHIEFY.
OH, BOY! WHAT UM TARGET!
NO-O-O! STOP!
I DID! BUT WHAT HAPPENED CHIEFY!
I WAS WADDLING ALONG UM ROAD WHEN
SO- HEH! HEH! HERE HE COMES!
PLUM! DID YOU BURN UM OLD CLOTHES? PLEASE SAY YOU DIDN'T!
NO "BUTS"!
ALL RIGHT, CHIEFY
I THINK HE'LL BE BACK SOON!
DON'T YOU THINK UM NEW CLOTHES ARE TOO TIGHT, CHIEFY?
DON'T BE SILLY UM CUSTOMER'S ALWAYS RIGHT! NOW BURN UM OLD CLOTHES!
BUT
CREAK!
LAKEDALE LEATHER
SO- THANKS FOR UM OTHER CLOTHES, PLUM! BUT I FEEL SILLY!
I'M SORRY CHIEFY, BUT THAT'S UM ONLY OUTFIT I HAVE THAT'LL FIT YOU!
OUCH! UM SHOES ARE KILLING ME!
ACME
TWINGE
WHOOPS! I'VE TORN UM HIPSTERS!
TEAR!
HEH! HEH! MISSED BY UM MILE!
13.8.66
LATER-
CHIEFY'S DONE ME UM GOOD TURN. SEE - HE'S STARTED UM NEW FASHION! EVERYBODY'S BUYING UM CLOTHES FROM MY SHOP!
'60s

'60s
1.3.69
Minnie the Minx
DAD, CAN I GET THAT?
CERTAINLY, MINNIE.
EMBROIDERY
WOODWORKER
SET
SO—
WHAT A SUPER PARENT I'VE GOT!
HOME—
I CAN'T WAIT TO GET MY HANDS ON THIS...
RIP!
TEAR
...EMBROIDERY SET?
YES, AND YOU'RE GOING TO USE IT...
EMBROIDERY FOR YOUNG LADIES
...OR ELSE! IT'LL KEEP YOU OUT OF MISCHIEF.
WHAT A ROTTEN PARENT I'VE GOT!
SO—
LET'S SEE WHAT YOU'VE DONE, MINNIE.
OK, DAD!
I HATE EMBROIDERY
NO-MORE-NONSENSE!
HUH! DAD'S GOT NO SENSE OF HUMOUR!
THUNK!
THUNK!
Minnie's attempts at embroidery should have you in stitches – although Dad soon realises she'd like to jacket in, when he becomes one of the 'flower people' of the '60s!
SO—
MUTTER! MUTTER!
TEE! HEE! HEE!
WHAT'S HE GIGGLING AT?

HA! HA! HA! HA! HO!
FUNNY!

THEN—
HEY! LOOK AT OLD SOFTY!
HAR! HAR!
IT'S ME THEY'RE LAUGHING AT!
HAW! HAW!
ROAD UP
ROAD

SCREAM!

JACKET INSIDE OUT →

LATER—
ARE YOU GOING TO EMBROIDER ALL THESE, MINNIE?
READER'S VOICE
NO!

LIKE I SAID IN PICTURE EIGHT—DAD'S GOT NO SENSE OF HUMOUR! OOYAH! WHAT A WHACKING THAT WAS!

'60s
Biffo's cooked up a little problem for himself. But, look — HAT'S the way to solve it!
BIFFO THE BEAR
COFFEE
I'D BETTER MIX UP THE CREAM FOR THE CREAM BUNS!
COFFEE
TEA
CREAM BUNS
HOT DOGS
HAMBURGERS
OUCH! CREAM IN MY EYE!
PESKY CREAM! OOPS! IT'S TIME I TURNED THE HAMBURGERS
SIZZLE!
SPIT!
EEK! STUNG WITH HOT FAT NOW!
SPLAT!
LATER—
OOYAH! MY NOSE AGAIN — SCALDED BY HOT COFFEE THIS TIME!
SUGAR
COFFEE
SPLASH!
I'VE HAD JUST ABOUT ENOUGH OF THIS!
GENTS' OUTFITTERS
I WANT TO CHANGE THIS CHEF'S HAT YOU SOLD ME YESTERDAY FOR ANOTHER ONE — SIZE 10!
S-SIZE 10, SIR? THAT'D BE FAR TOO BIG FOR YOU!
YOU HEARD — SIZE 10!
BACK AT THE STALL —
HOW'S THIS FOR ALL-ROUND PROTECTION, CHUMS?
SIZZLE
SPIT!
20.10.62

This isn't exactly a fashion story of the '60s, but was chosen to let you see what Dennis looks like when he's wearing something other than a striped jumper!

THE BASH STREET KIDS
SPRING WILL BE HERE SOON! TRA-LA-LA!
HOW NICE IT WILL BE TO SEE THE BUDDING OF MOTHER NATURE- THE BEAUTY OF THE FRESH COUNTRYSIDE UNFOLDING ITSELF FOR ANOTHER YEAR! SIGH!
SNIFF! SNIFF!
AT SCHOOL -
LOOK OUT, ERBERT! HERE'S TEACHER NOW!
Teacher
DID YOU DO THAT?
ER-YES, TEACHER!
HM! IT SHOWS A CERTAIN AMOUNT OF TALENT -
LATER, IN THE CLASSROOM -
WHAT ON EARTH ARE YOU DOING SMIFFY?
THAT'S A BIT OF POP-ART, TEACHER!
POP!
IT'S JUST A SMALL STAIN, JANITOR.
AARGH! MY LOVELY CLEAN WALL!

You'd think that the Bash Street Kids would be the last to know anything about 'pop art' — originated by Andy Warhol back in the Sixties — but maybe Smiffy knows more than he is telling (see pic 14!).

1.3.69

Here are a couple of stories with a twist – no, not an unexpected ending, but one of the dance crazes of the Sixties!

MINNIE THE MINX

LITTLE PLUM

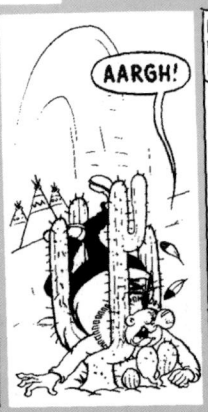

2.6.62

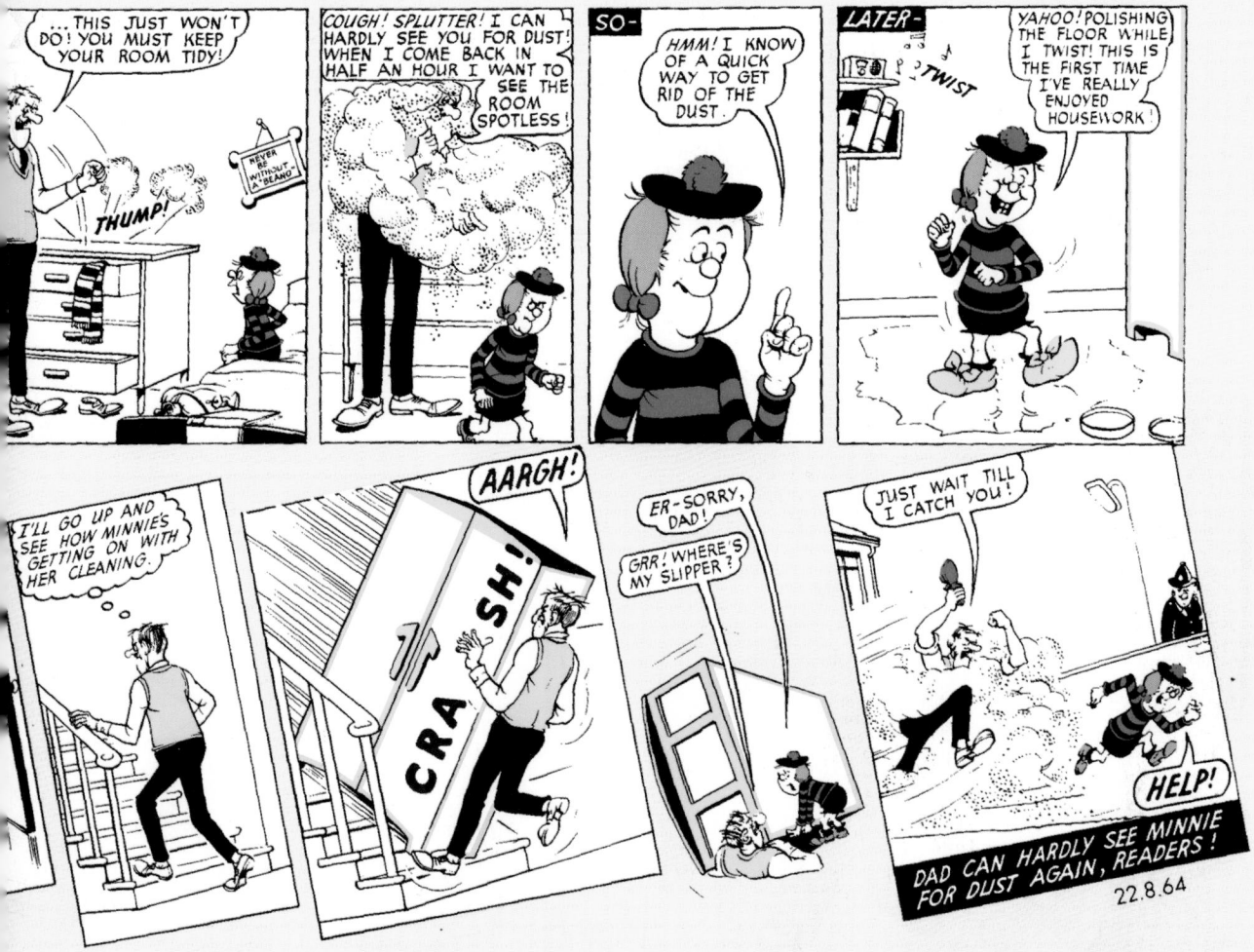
...THIS JUST WON'T DO! YOU MUST KEEP YOUR ROOM TIDY!
THUMP!
NEVER BE WITHOUT A BRAND
COUGH! SPLUTTER! I CAN HARDLY SEE YOU FOR DUST! WHEN I COME BACK IN HALF AN HOUR I WANT TO SEE THE ROOM SPOTLESS!
SO-
HMM! I KNOW OF A QUICK WAY TO GET RID OF THE DUST.
LATER-
TWIST
YAHOO! POLISHING THE FLOOR WHILE I TWIST! THIS IS THE FIRST TIME I'VE REALLY ENJOYED HOUSEWORK!
I'LL GO UP AND SEE HOW MINNIE'S GETTING ON WITH HER CLEANING.
AARGH!
CRA SH!
ER-SORRY, DAD!
GRR! WHERE'S MY SLIPPER?
JUST WAIT TILL I CATCH YOU!
HELP!
DAD CAN HARDLY SEE MINNIE FOR DUST AGAIN, READERS!
22.8.64

UM GRAND OL' DUKE OF YORK, HE HAD TEN...
OW-OO-OO! OUCH-OOW!
UM DANCE ENDS-
THANK YOU, CHIEF! YOU DANCE DIVINELY!
THROB
THROB
NOW TAKE YOUR PARTNERS FOR UM BARN DANCE.
UM TWO CHIEFS LINK ARMS AND TWIRL-
SCREECH!

IT'S UM GOOD JOB UM TRIBE LEARNED HOW TO DO UM "TWIST." IT'S UM ONLY WAY TO DODGE UM MISSILES!
IF I UM EVER GET OUT OF THIS, I'LL TWIST PLUM'S NECK!
UM AARGH!

The use of robot soldiers may seem fashionable today, but it isn't a modern idea — or a very good one, if you put a certain Corporal Clott, from the Dandy, in charge of the robot!
THIS IS ONE OF THE NEW ROBOTS I'VE INVENTED FOR THE ARMY, COLONEL. IT'S SO SIMPLE TO WORK THAT IT CAN BE OPERATED BY EVEN THE DIMMEST SOLDIER.
IS THAT SO? WELL, JUST A MOMENT . . .
CORPORAL CLOTT! COME HERE!
LOOK AT MY UNIFORM, CLOTT! IT'S DUSTY.
THE ROBOT WILL DUST YOU DOWN, SIR!
I'LL TRY THESE SWITCHES.
YIKES! PUT ME DOWN!
AH! HERE'S TODAY'S PAPER. MUST CATCH UP WITH THE NEWS!
THE ROBOT HAS FINISHED PEELING THE POTATOES AND NOW LOOKS FOR SOMETHING ELSE TO PEEL . . .
OH, DEAR! HOW DID THAT HAPPEN?
YOU FOOL, CLOTT! IT'S SMASHED MY TELLY!
I'LL TURN THE SWITCH THE OTHER WAY. OOPS! TOO FAR AGAIN!
GIVE ME THAT CONTROL BOX, CLOTT, AND— TAKE THAT!
THE BOX IS BROKEN, AND TH ROBOT IS OUT OF CONTROL!
YELP! I'M GOING TO BE SKEWERED ALIVE!

NOW THAT I'VE SHOWN THE CORPORAL HOW IT WORKS, HE CAN HAVE A GO.
FETCH POLISH AND BRUSHES, CLOTT. I WANT MY BOOTS CLEANED.
RIGHT, SIR.
CLOTT RETURNS–
READY, SIR? WELL, HERE GOES– OOPS!
ARGH! LET GO!
GOSH! I DON'T SEEM TO HAVE GOT THE HANG OF THIS CONTROL BOX!
GET THIS TIN MENACE OFF MY BACK AT ONCE, CLOTT!
'60s
GRR! THAT METAL MENACE HAS RUINED MY UNIFORM WITH THOSE BOOT BRUSHES.
NEVER MIND, COLONEL! LET THE CORPORAL DEMONSTRATE THE ROBOT DOING KITCHEN DUTIES.
HOW'S THAT, SIR? THE ROBOT CAN PEEL POTATOES FASTER THAN ANY MAN IN THE CAMP.
SO IT CAN! PERHAPS WE CAN FIND A USE FOR IT AFTER ALL.
THE ROBOT WILL MAKE A VERY GOOD SENTRY, COLONEL.
ALL RIGHT! WE'LL FETCH A RIFLE AND PUT IT THROUGH ITS PACES.
WHAT ON EARTH! THE ROBOT HAS PEELED PACKETS OF SOAP POWDER, TEA AND CHOCOLATE–ALL INTO ONE HORRIBLE LOOKING HEAP.
AT THE COLONEL'S HOME–
LET THE CORPORAL DEMONSTRATE HOW GOOD A SENTRY THE ROBOT IS, COLONEL.
OOPS! I'VE TURNED THE SWITCH TOO FAR.
OH, NO! MY NEW SIDEBOARD!
I THINK I CAN REPAIR THIS! FETCH ME A SCREWDRIVER, CORPORAL!
NEVER MIND A SCREWDRIVER! FETCH A SLEDGEHAMMER TO MASH THIS METAL MENACE INTO SCRAP!
16.3.68

The fashion in the Dandy of the 'Sixties was for squirty flowers and exploding cigars — but it could also predict fashionable things for the future! Look at the third-last picture of this Big Head and Thick Head story and you'll spot an absolutely 'wizard' name!

A BEANO ~~WEEK~~

There's no room in this book for a Beano Calendar — they didn't go on sale until the 1980s — but here's a week's-worth of Beano stories from the '60s. Stop day-dreaming, and start day-reading!

GUMDAY

26.8.67

MUGSDAY

8.7.67

ZOOSDAY

THE
BASH STREET KIDS

NO! NO! PLEASE NOT THAT, HEADMASTER!
PLEASE! NO! NO!
BONK! BONK!
NO! NO! MERCY!

NO! NO! PLEASE DON'T MAKE ME TAKE THE BASH ST. KIDS TO THE ZOO — LAST TIME I TOOK THEM THEY LOCKED ME INTO THE CROCODILE HOUSE JUST WHEN THEY WERE DUE TO BE FED — NO! NO! CROCS. PLEASE NOT THAT! MERCY!
BONK BONK

WHAT A FUSS ABOUT NOTHING! I'LL TAKE THEM TO THE ZOO!
ELEFUNT
CROCODILE

COME ALONG, CHILDREN—WE'LL HAVE A LOOK AT THE POLAR BEARS.
ZOO CAFE
POLAR BEARS
MAIN ENTRANCE
AFRICAN ANIMALS
HAVE A CARROT!

INSIDE THE ENCLOSURE DANNY TRIES HIS HAND AT ELEPHANT TRAINING.
COME ON, ELEFUNT—IF HE CAN DO IT SO CAN YOU!

TO ARMS, KEEPERS! THE BASH ST. KIDS HAVE INVADED OUR ZOO.
HIPPO CATCHING NET
SNAKE NET

THE ZOO ATTENDANTS ARE COMING TO CATCH US, DANNY!
DON'T WORRY, I'LL FIX 'EM WITH THIS SNEEZING POWDER!
BASH ST. WILD WEST CAVALRY

CHOO!

HEH! HEH! RIGHT INTO THE SEAL POND!
CHOO!

I'LL FIX THOSE CHILDREN MYSELF.
ZOO AQUARIUM

GET 'EM, OLLY— I'LL GIVE YOU A BIG FEED AFTERWARDS!
ZOO AQUARIUM
HIMALAYAN WOOLY BEAR. DO NOT DISTURB HIBERNATING
ERK!
SOME HAIR-CREAM SMEARED ON THE ELEFUNT'S TRUNK MAKES A SMASHING SLIDE— ERK!
ELEPHANT CRUSH!
SNORE
LANDING CUSHION

GOOD OLD HEADMASTER! THE PUBLIC WILL PAY EXTRA TO SEE THIS LOT!
RARE WILD ANIMALS FROM BASH ST.
MISSING LINK BETWEEN HUMANS AND HEDGEHOGS
PORKUS GRUNTUS HALF PIG HALF WHALE
RARE ANIMAL CROSSED WITH BURST GAS BLOWER
PLUGORILLA

FISHINGSDAY

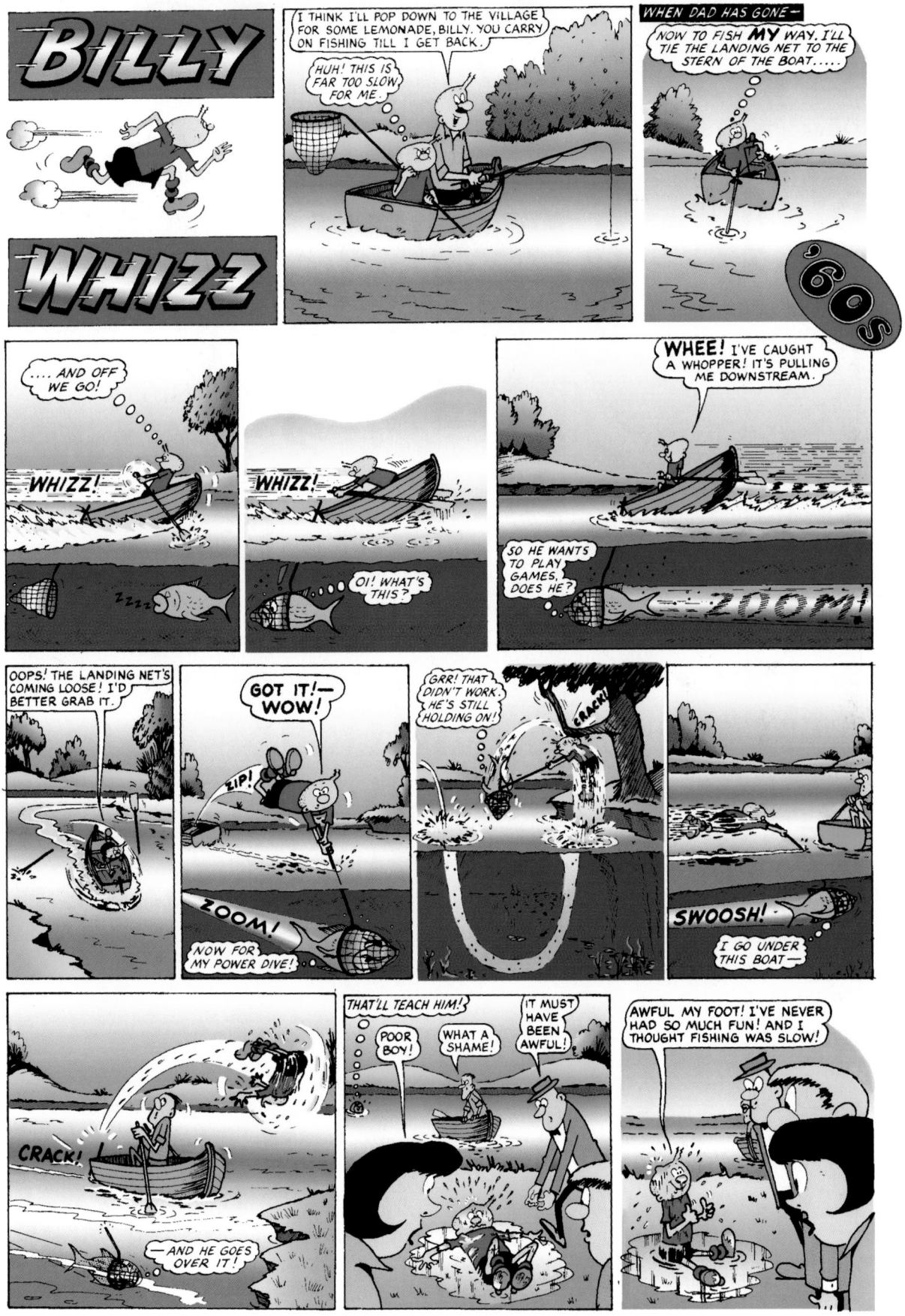

THIRSTDAY

2.12.67

FIGHTDAY

PUNCH and JIMMY

'60s

30.9.67

SCATTERDAY

30.9.67

Winker Watson

THE boys of the Third Form at Greytowers School were all very busy. They were washing their necks, polishing shoes, and generally sprucing themselves up – which was very unusual indeed. But then, today was the day when, along with the Third Form girls from Oak Lodge School next door, they had been invited to tea by the squire. However, at the last moment, Winker Watson, the champion wangler, heard that the girls wouldn't be going.

WHAT? MISS CREEP'S KEEPING YOU IN FOR EXTRA NEEDLEWORK ON YOUR HALF HOL? RIDICULOUS! WELL, WE'RE ALL READY TO GO TO SQUIRE DODD'S TREAT. HOPE YOU CAN MAKE IT SOMEHOW!

THIRD FORM CLOAK ROOM

WHAT A SHAME, WINKER! STILL ALL THE MORE FOR US TO EAT!

The boys set off for the feast, and Winker started up a rousing chorus. But that was a big mistake!

ALL TOGETHER, LADS... 'HEIGH-HO, HEIGH-HO, TO SQUIRE DODD'S WE GO!...

For their Form Master had not been invited, and he was so sour about that that he stopped the boys going!

STOP! I'M TAKING YOU BOYS TO THE ART GALLERY. VERY EDUCATIONAL!

BUT, MR CREEP, SIR, THIS IS OUR HALF-HOLIDAY!

FOLLOW ME, YOU BOYS!

IN YOU GO, SIR.

Fortunately, Winker was a pal of the bus conductor. Strange signs and winks passed between them.

My goodness! The conductor did ring the bell quickly. So quickly that Creepy was the only one to get aboard. Winker's signs had been understood!

HEE HEE!

OH, SIR! YOU'VE GONE WITHOUT US!

TING! TING!

TOWN

Alas, Winker's little wangle was wasted, for along came another of the masters in a big station wagon.

DON'T WORRY, LADS–I SAW THE BUS GO OFF WITHOUT YOU! BUT I'VE GOT PLENTY OF ROOM, SO JUMP IN AND WE'LL SOON CATCH UP WITH MR CREEP!

TRUST OLD STINKS TO COME OUT OF SCHOOL RIGHT NOW!...

ER, THANK YOU, SIR, IF YOU INSIST!

Once at the art gallery, most of the lads felt like saying goodbye to the squire's party. But not Winker!

WASTE OF A HALF HOL, WINKER.

FOLLOW ME CLOSELY, BOYS, AND NO DODGING OFF!

CHEER UP, TROTTY, IT'S NOT WASTED YET!

ART GALLERY

TO THE MAIN HALL

INFORMATION BUREAU

Winker's first move was to start improving the art in the gallery.

THERE! I ALWAYS RECKONED OLD JULIUS SNEEZER WOULD LOOK BETTER WITH A 'TASH!

Tim Trott joined in before Winker produced a catapult for Stage Two of his plan.

IF THE JANITOR WANTS HIS BUCKET, WINKER, TELL HIM OLD NEPTUNE'S GOT IT! HEE HEE!

TELL HIM YOURSELF, TROTTY–I'M TAKING A POT-SHOT AT OLD CREEPY!

Bull's eye! The master's mortar board was whipped off his head!

YOW! HOW DID THAT HAPPEN?

GUIDE BOOK

And it landed on top of an Egyptian Mummy, where Creepy was caught trying to retrieve it.

OHO! SO YOU'RE THE ONE WHO'S BEEN FOOLING ABOUT WITH THE WORKS OF ART! COME DOWN AT ONCE, YOU VANDAL!

ER, BELIEVE IT OR NOT, MY GOOD MAN, BUT I'M ONLY TRYING TO GET MY HAT BACK!

Winker's cunning plan had worked! They were all being turfed out.

EXIT

OUT YOU GO, AND TAKE YOUR BOYS WITH YOU BEFORE THEY START FOLLOWING YOUR HORRIBLE EXAMPLE!

WE'RE KEEPING CLOSE BEHIND YOU LIKE YOU SAID, SIR!

YOU BOYS GET ON THE BUS FIRST THIS TIME, HURRY NOW...

PSST! STAY JAMMED IN THE DOORWAY, LADS!

Winker's idea now was to get away from Mr Creep. And this was how he worked it.

SORRY, CHUM! THERE'S HARDLY ROOM FOR THIS LOT! NEXT BUS!

...BUT THAT'S NOT FOR AN HOUR!

The wangle had worked! Old Creepy was left behind this time.

But the master wasn't stuck. The Headmistress of Oak Lodge was his sister, and she would help him out.

I KNOW! I'LL PHONE SISTER AGNES, AND ASK HER TO COME AND FETCH ME!

VEGETABLES

GOOD JOB I JUMPED OFF THE BUS AGAIN! NOW I CAN FIND OUT WHAT CREEPY'S UP TO...

IT'S TOO BAD OF YOU, CLARENCE! I'VE HAD TO LEAVE MY GIRLS ON THEIR OWN TO COME AND COLLECT YOU!

That was too bad – but worse was to follow after the watching Winker had done his stuff!

A SPUD IN THE EXHAUST PIPE SHOULD DO THE TRICK!

While Creepy gazed helplessly at the engine Winker sped off to make a couple of phone calls before heading for Oak Lodge.

?

IT MUST BE YOUR FAULT THAT IT WON'T GO, CLARENCE!

OKAY, GIRLS, MISS CREEP IS OUT OF THE WAY, SO OFF WE GO TO SQUIRE DODD'S DO!

SCHOOL FOR GIRLS MR CREEP

Winker was hailed like a hero. And that is exactly what he was, of course!

The squire's party had just begun when two furious and unsuccessful motor mechanics burst in.

?

JUST LOOK AT THESE GREEDY BRATS OF OURS, AGNES!... DISGRACEFUL GOINGS ON!

22.6.68

But the two Creeps got a shock. They hadn't expected the Head to be here! Winker's wangles had all turned up trumps again!

CREEP–AND YOU, TOO, MISS CREEP! HOW DARE YOU GATE-CRASH THE SQUIRE'S PARTY SO RUDELY! RETURN TO YOUR DUTIES AT ONCE!

I SHOULD JOLLY WELL THINK SO, 'OO, HEADMASTER!

OO-ER! RUN FOR IT, AGNES!

JOLLY GOOD IDEA OF YOURS GETTING THE SQUIRE TO INVITE THE HEAD AT THE LAST MOMENT, WINKER!

The Dandy's hovercraft story, seven years before The Beano strip seen earlier in this book, was

The HOVERCAR SNATCHERS

an evil tale of masked men, a kidnapped footballer, and a beautifully-drawn steam train!

6.1.62

Here's a rather unusual wartime invention from

THE WOODEN SUBMARINE

MIKE and Ella Trubb were listening along with their Dad to the strangest escape plan ever proposed. Mr Trubb was an oil engineer in Borneo, which was being invaded by Japanese armies.

A Borneo barrelmaker called Seesaw had drawn up plans to build a wooden submarine, and in this remarkable craft, he told the Trubbs, they might escape to Australia!

Dad agreed—but very unwillingly. He doubted if the flimsy wooden craft could survive such a perilous voyage. Still, Seesaw set to work, aided by Mike and Ella, and the unusual craft soon began to take shape.

Already the Japanese were within striking distance. One of their planes zoomed over the harbour, gunning the Wooden Submarine.

Fortunately, Seesaw was able to repair the damage done by the bullets, but next day more raiders came. In a desperate attempt to prevent the submarine being holed again, Seesaw launched his craft—but that was a mistake!

Leaking badly, the submarine listed to one side then sank. Seesaw leaped clear! It seemed his clever invention was doomed.

People were leaving the island in all manner of boats. Now that the wooden sub was out of action, Mr Trubb hustled his children aboard the last junk. He would stay behind, but the youngsters must take their chance to escape.

Dandy 1969 — but WOOD it really work?

8.11.69

DING-DONG! DING-DONG! HEAR YE! HEAR YE! On this day there will be peals of laughter

when you bellow out loud at the batty antics of Brassneck the metal boy, from June 1967.

3.6.67

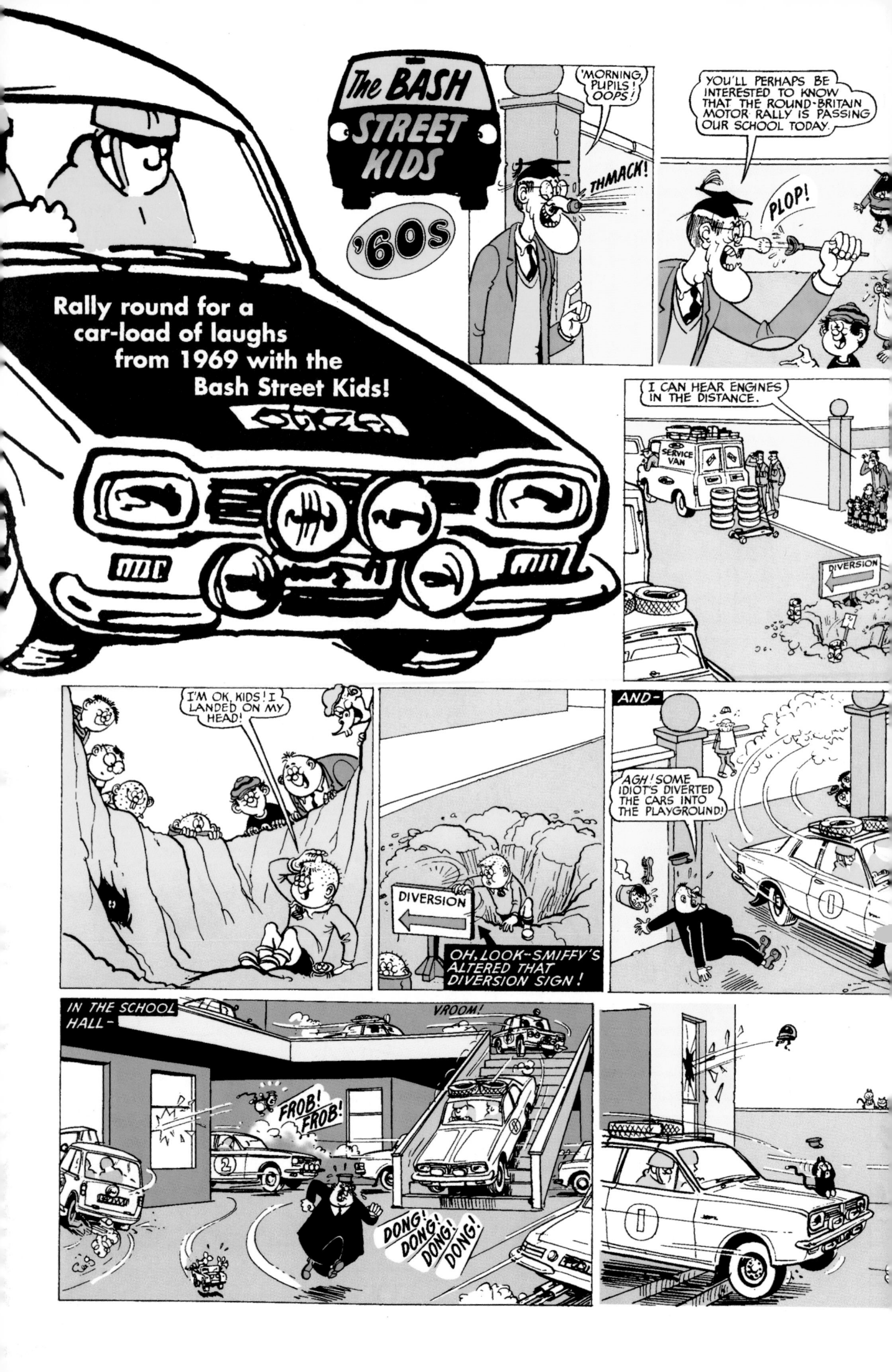
The BASH STREET KIDS
'60s
Rally round for a car-load of laughs from 1969 with the Bash Street Kids!
'MORNING, PUPILS! OOPS!
THMACK!
YOU'LL PERHAPS BE INTERESTED TO KNOW THAT THE ROUND-BRITAIN MOTOR RALLY IS PASSING OUR SCHOOL TODAY.
PLOP!
I CAN HEAR ENGINES IN THE DISTANCE.
SERVICE VAN
DIVERSION
I'M OK, KIDS! I LANDED ON MY HEAD!
DIVERSION
OH, LOOK-SMIFFY'S ALTERED THAT DIVERSION SIGN!
AND-
AGH! SOME IDIOT'S DIVERTED THE CARS INTO THE PLAYGROUND!
IN THE SCHOOL HALL-
VROOM!
FROB! FROB!
DONG! DONG! DONG! DONG!

AH, I WELL REMEMBER MY RALLY-DRIVING DAYS!
FROB!
I WAS A LEADING RALLY DRIVER, KNOWN AS TEARAWAY TEACHER, THE TERROR OF THE TRACK!
IS THAT A FACT?
I HEREBY DECLARE A HALF-DAY SO WE CAN WATCH THE CARS GO BY!
WHOOPEE! GOOD OLD TEARAWAY TEACHER!
HEY, MISTER! YOUR WATCH HAS ONLY GOT ONE HAND!
MARSHALL
IT'S A STOP-WATCH, BUFFOON! IT'S ONLY SUPPOSED TO HAVE ONE HAND!
GADOING!
MIND THAT HOLE, SMIFFY!
DIVERSION
WHAT HOLE?
CRASH!
!
DIVERS
ROAR!
VRUUMM!
HELP! HEAD TEACHER! SAVE ME!
HEH-HEH! TEARAWAY TEACHER'S LEADING THE RALLY, JUST LIKE THE OLD DAYS!
WRUMM!
5.4.69

26.7.69
"Mule" like this Little Plum story from 1969!
DRRING!
HO-HUM! TIME TO GET UP.
YAWN! THAT'S UM NICE HERD OF...
CLICK!
...MULES?
SO–
M-MULES IN UM WIGWAM!
YES—I'VE DECIDED TO GO INTO UM TRANSPORT BUSINESS WITH UM MULE TRAIN. IT'S YOUR JOB TO TEACH UM MULES ALL ABOUT IT.
LATER–
HYUP!
STAND
STILL
MOVE, YOU SILLY ASSES!
STAND
STILL
THEN–
IDEA!
WHOOOOOOOO!
LOOK—THERE'S UM OTHER KIND OF TRAIN YOU MUST DO WHAT IT DOES, SEE?
PLEASE MOVE! I'M SORRY I CALLED YOU "SILLY"!
SO –
WHOOOOOO!
I GIVE UP!
SO–
WHAT'S WRONG, PLUM?
I'LL TELL YOU...
...UM MULE TRAIN JUST WON'T BE TRAINED! I TRIED TO TRAIN UM MULE TRAIN, BUT EVEN UM TRAIN COULDN'T TRAIN UM MULE TRAIN—SO I GIVE UP!
I GIVE UP, TOO!
STRAIN
'60s

BIFFO THE BEAR
I'M OFF FOR A WINTER HOLIDAY IN THE MOUNTAINS.
O-O-O-O-O! THIS MOUNTAIN ROAD'S MAKING ME SEASICK!
SWAY
LURCH
BUMP!
DOH-H-H-H! I FEEL TERRIBLE, BUT I EXPECT A BRISK SKI-RUN WILL PUT ME RIGHT!
'60s
The Beano's favourite bear was following a new trend when he decided to have a winter holiday, back in December 1962 — but 'Biffo-re' he could have much fun, he suffered a touch of ski-sickness!
GULP! WHAT A SWITCHBACK!
GROO-H-I-I-A! I FEEL MORE SEASICK THAN EVER. BUT, IF I CAN'T SKI, I'LL HAVE TO FIND SOMETHING ELSE TO PASS THE TIME.
AND SO —
WOULD YOU BELIEVE IT? THE ONLY PLACE I DON'T GET SEASICK AROUND HERE IS ON WATER!

15.12.62

'60s
DENNIS the MENACE
I'M TAKING YOU ON A VISIT TO THE ZOO. GO AND GET YOUR JACKETS.
THE ZOO! GOOD! MAYBE I'LL GET A LION AS A PET.
DENNIS, YOU WILL REMAIN IN SCHOOL AND DO EXTRA SUMS BECAUSE YOU'VE BEEN NAUGHTY!
BAH!
IN THE CLOAKROOM—
I'LL GET TO THE ZOO YET! WALTER WILL HELP ME.
HOW'S THIS FOR A DISGUISE, READERS?
SLAM
!
I'LL COME BACK AND LET YOU OUT AFTER THE ZOO VISIT, WALTER!
THEN—
AH, WALTER! NOW WE'RE ALL HERE, WE'LL START WITH A RIDE ON THE ELEPHANT.
HUH! THIS ELEPHANT'S TOO SLOW. THEY'RE SUPPOSED TO BE SCARED OF MICE. MAYBE THIS WILL SPEED IT UP.
EEK! A MOUSE!
HELP! MUMMY!
THIS IS MORE LIKE IT.
MEANWHILE—
OFFICE
EEK! STOP THIEF! COME BACK WITH THE ZOO TAKINGS!
LET'S GO, HORACE!
BUT—
GET THAT ELEPHANT OUT OF THE WAY! WE WANT TO ESCAPE!
WHEN THE POLICE ARRIVE—
POLICE
IT WAS WALTER'S IDEA TO USE THE ELEPHANT TO BLOCK THE ALLEY.
IT'S TIME I WAS OUT OF HERE!
NEXT DAY—
TAKE THIS REWARD, YOU BRAVE BOY!
B-BUT I DIDN'T DO ANYTHING, SIR!
SUCH A MODEST LITTLE FELLOW!
An elephant played a BIG part in this Walter the S . . . sorry, Dennis the Menace story from 1966!
30.7.66.

'60s
BIFFO THE BEAR
WHY DON'T YOU COME ALONG TO THE SCOOTER RALLY, BIFFO?
I HAVEN'T GOT A SCOOTER, BUT I'LL TRY TO BORROW ONE.
BIFFO
NOW, WHERE CAN I GET A SCOOTER?
YOU CAN BORROW OUR HORACE'S SCOOTER, BIFFO!
COO! THANKS, MRS BLOGGS!
AT THE RALLY–
WONDER IF BIFFO WILL MAKE IT?
OH, NO!
'BLUSH'
JUDGE
HA-HA-HA!
The speed record for motor scooters is thought to be held by an English woman who in 1965 ran her 200 cc Lambretta at over 130 mph on a racetrack at Monza, Italy. Perhaps Biffo won't scoot along so swiftly!
NEVER MIND, BIFFO, I'M AWARDING YOU A SPECIAL PRIZE FOR THE BEST NOVELTY ENTRANT.
914 KPL

THE amazing story of William Grange, a schoolboy who has a secret identity — that of Billy the Cat, the mysterious crime-fighter of Burnham. One evening Billy is patrolling the rooftops of the town when a voice hails him from the street below...

In the Beano of 1969, the towns of Burnham and Blackcastle must be within easy reach of each other, because the Hovertank's owner, Mr Knight, who lives in Blackcastle, has an urgent meeting with Billy the Cat in his home town of Burnham —

29.3.69

HERE IT IS!
Billy knew the men. They were Stan Lawson and Bert Gibb, part of a gang of crooks run by Alan Robb.

'60s
As the Hovertank left, Billy jumped up from cover.

He dropped, silently, on to the turret.

Soon, the Hovertank reached its destination—a hut far out on Burnham Moor.

The two messengers were greeted by the other members of the gang, Sandy Baird and Alan Robb himself.
GOT THE CASH, EH?

Suddenly—
B-BILLY THE CAT!

Baird swung his fist, but . . .

. . . he was no match for a judo expert like Billy the Cat!
COME ON, KID—WE'RE GETTING OUT OF HERE!

Robb bundled Kevin into the Hovertank and started the motors and, at the roar of the jets, Billy rushed outside . . .
. . . but he was too late.

As the Hovertank raced out of the gully, Billy ran for the steep hillside.
By taking a short cut over the hill, Billy had got ahead of the stolen Hovertank.
GOOD! HERE IT COMES!
But, just as Billy was about to jump on the Hovertank, Robb spotted him.
Robb put the Hovertank into a swerve so that Billy missed.
Then the machine swung completely round and charged at Billy . . .
But Robb had forgotten about Billy's wonderful agility.
The crook panicked . . .

He jumped from the fast-moving vehicle.

HI, KEVIN — SOON HAVE YOU FREE!

But the Hovertank had stampeded a herd of cattle . . .
GET TO THE CONTROLS, KEVIN!
SWING THE TURRET ROUND!
H-HELP!
. . . and Robb was directly in their path!

Billy had grabbed the crook in the nick of time.

Meanwhile, Tom Knight, designer of the famous Hovertank and father of the twins, had told the Burnham police about the kidnapping and Billy's rescue attempt.
WE'LL HAVE TO SEARCH THE WHOLE MOOR!

Suddenly—
LOOK!
Billy and Kevin had returned to the crooks' hut on the moor, freed Kenneth and brought the kidnappers back.

Shortly after, Billy was home changing to his other identity, that of William Grange, a seemingly quiet schoolboy.

Next day, at Burnham Academy—
THE HOVERTANK WAS IN TOWN TODAY WITH BILLY THE CAT, WILLIAM — PITY YOU MISSED THEM!
ER-YES!

'60s
Minnie the Minx and dressmaking don't mix in this 1967 tale — until she gets an idea from another Beano character that "suits" her!
Down below, the Bash Street Pups have a similar idea . . . meet 'Sniffy the Cat'!
DOMESTIC SCIENCE CLASS AT SCHOOL—
DRESSMAKING TODAY, PUPILS.
GOODY!
I JUST LOVE DRESSMAKING!
SUPER!
WHAT DOES MINNIE THINK OF DRESSMAKING?
YECH!
29.3.69
HARD THINKS
Come on, you lot—think hard! We've got to do something funny for our "Beano" artist to draw this week.
I KNOW!
I'll be Sniffy the—I mean BILLY THE CAT, and you lot can be the crooks!
SO—
AIYIEEE!
DUH! WHO THREW THAT TREE AT ME?
KRUMP!
LATER—
Guess what Tubby's supposed to be!
The HOVERTANK, of course!
Well, you'll just have to find yourselves another HOVERTANK—my tum's sore!
BOING!
BOING!
SEE THE HOVERTANK ELSEWHERE IN THE BOOK.

SO—
THAT'S RIGHT, GIRLS—MAKE SURE THE HEM'S RIGHT BEFORE YOU STITCH IT.
THEN—
YOWL!
YOU STICK THE PINS IN THE DRESS, FOOLISH GIRL—NOT ME!
SO—
THAT'S FINE, MAVIS.
GRR! WHAT KIND OF STITCH IS THAT SUPPOSED TO BE?
LATER, AT HOME—
YOUR TEACHER PHONED, MINNIE—SHE SAID YOU NEEDED SOME DRESSMAKING PRACTICE, SO HERE'S SOME MATERIAL...
OH, NO!
...AND HERE'S A NICE LITTLE FROCK YOU CAN MAKE.
SOPPY FROCK—I'D RATHER MAKE A "BILLY THE CAT" SUIT!
LATER—
HOW DO YOU LIKE IT, READERS?
"Beano" Reader's Voice
WHERE DID YOU GET THE LEATHER?
THEN—
COME HERE, GIRL!
GULP!
LOOK AT THAT—MY FAVOURITE CHAIR!
WELL, YOUNG LADY, THERE'S JUST ENOUGH LEATHER LEFT ON THE CHAIR FOR WHAT I WANT TO MAKE!
WHACK!
OW!
OW!
WHACK!
CAN YOU GUESS WHAT DAD MADE?

25.11.67

'60s
Thanks to Billy the Cat, you've met Sniffy the Cat. Now meet . . . Dennis the Dog!
DENNIS MENACE
COO! BILLY THE CAT'S SUPER! HE'S GIVEN ME AN IDEA.
FIRST I NEED MY ZIP-UP WINTER PYJAMAS THAT I'VE ALWAYS HATED.
A DAB HERE AND A DAB THERE.
NOW DAD'S CRASH HELMET, SUITABLY DECORATED.
YOU'VE HEARD OF BILLY THE CAT—
NOW MEET DENNIS THE DOG! GRR!
I'LL HAVE THAT JUICY LEG OF CHICKEN: TA!
YIPE!
SHOVE
HEH! HEH! A DOGS LIFE IS GREAT! SLURP!
I SHALL INFORM HIS PARENT AT ONCE!
WHIMPER!
LATER, WALTER'S ON HIS WAY HOME —
GRR!
I DO HOPE THERE ARE NO NASTY DOGS ABOUT. I'M SCARED OF DOGS!
TREMBLE
SNARL! GNASH! GURR! ROWF!
SHRIEK! MUMSIE, SAVE ME!
THEN—
WATCH ME SCARE THAT CAT.
SNUG
GRR! SNARL! ERK!
GOT YOU, YOU PESKY PUP. THAT'S ONLY A TOY CAT!
SNATCH
SO—
HOME, DENNIS. IT'S TIME FOR "WALKIES", OR SHOULD I SAY "WHACKIES"!
SURELY YOU WOULDN'T HIT A POOR DUMB ANIMAL, DAD!

19.8.67

Here's another Billy the Cat tale. Well, it is but it isn't . . . it's Billy the Whizz Cat acting like a Mole! Is this all too fast for you, readers? Oh, just read the story!

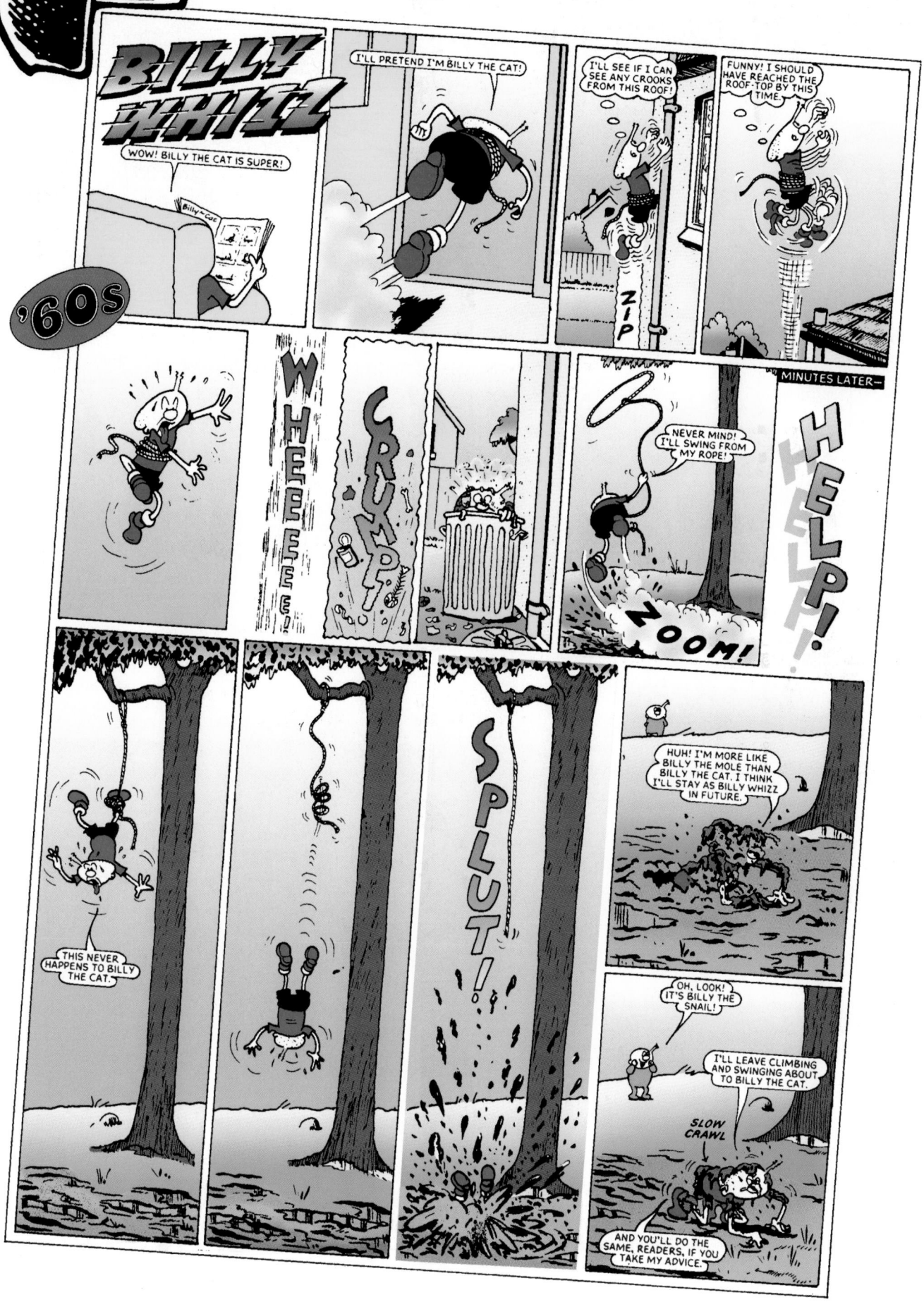

Here's a confusing one! Visiting the Three Bears' page are — the Three Bears!
'60s
29.4.67
LET'S GO AND RAID HANK'S STORE.
BUT—
NOW TO GET YOU FOR RAIDING MY STORE THIS MORNING!
EH?
BUT HANK, WE WEREN'T NEAR YOUR STORE THIS MORNING.
BACK AT THE CAVE—
LET'S GO AND COLLECT THAT PIE WE ORDERED FROM GREEDY GULCH BAKERY.
AT THE BAKERY—
BUT YOU COLLECTED THE PIE AN HOUR AGO, PA!
DID HE?
THERE'S SOMETHING FUNNY GOING ON HERE!
SUDDENLY—
AARGH! IT'S US.
GURR! IT'S GRIZZLY GUS AND HIS FAMILY IN DISGUISE! LET'S GET THEM!
THEN—
AHEM! WHICH OF YOU ARE "THE THREE BEARS"?
GASP! WE ARE!
HUMPH! YOU DON'T LOOK MUCH LIKE BEARS TO ME!
AAH! YOU THREE LOOK MORE LIKE "THE THREE BEARS". AS SECRETARY OF THE BEANO SUPPORTERS CLUB I AM AUTHORISED TO INVITE YOU TO A BUMPER TUCK-IN!
COO!
IT WAS YOUR FAULT!
NO! IT WAS YOUR FAULT!
TO THE FEAST.

A certain bargain hunter was only 28 years old, and not yet famous, when this 'antique' Beano Cover was published. No — his face wasn't on the original cover!

Here's a puzzle for you — how did the guest on Plum's page get to Plum's village? Think fast!
LITTLE PLUM
NICE AND QUIET
EEK!
ZOOOM-M!
YOW!
WHEE-EEE!
THUD!
'60s
SORRY, PLUM!
WH-WHAT HAPPENED?
I PASSED YOU ON UM NEW MOTOR-BIKE — IT DOES UM HUNDRED AND TWENTY MILES UM HOUR!
HUMPH!
LATER-
MUST GET THESE EGGS TO THE LUMBER CAMP
NO, CHIEFY! STOP!
EGGS
BRR!
YIPES!
ZOOM!
THAT BIKE'S UM MENACE — IT MUST GO!
SO -
....HERE'S WHAT I WANT YOU TO DO....
I'VE GOT SOMEONE WHO'LL TAKE YOU FOR UM REALLY FAST RUN.
SUPER!
COME ON, CHIEFY!
LIFT-T
VROOO-OOM!
HELP! WHOA! CEASE! HALT! STOP!
VROO-OOM!
GOSH! IT'S BILLY WHIZZ!
LATER-
LIKE UM LIFT BACK TO UM VILLAGE, CHIEFY?
N-NO, THANKS! THAT HORSE IS TOO FAST FOR ME NOW!
25.11.67

A DANDY
WEEK
WEAK WITH LAUGHTER!
No body should be without happy memories — so here's a week's-worth of Dandy stories from the '60s, which older readers may recall and younger readers can enjoy tattoo . . . er . . . too!
THE DANDY

NUTSDAY

9.1.65

NOMONEYDAY

22.6.68

TATTOOSDAY

Dirty DICK
HOW DO YOU LIKE MY TATTOOS, DICK?
GOSH! THEY'RE SUPER!
I'LL HAVE A GO AT TATTOOING MYSELF WITH MY BALL-POINT PEN. LOOK, THAT'S NOT BAD! I'LL TRY A FEW MORE.
HI, MUM AND DAD! HOW DO YOU LIKE MY DO-IT-YOURSELF TATTOOS?
GET UPSTAIRS AT ONCE, DICK, AND INTO THE BATH!
DICK! FANCY SCRIBBLING ALL OVER YOURSELF LIKE THAT!
'60s
IT'S GOING TO TAKE SOME SCRUBBING TO GET THIS MESS OFF!
OW! YOW! OOYAH!
BAH! DAD SCRUBBED ME SO HARD, I'M TINGLING ALL OVER! I'LL HAVE TO THINK OF A WAY OF GETTING BETTER TATTOOS—THE KIND MUM AND DAD MIGHT LIKE.
JOHNNY'S TOP OF MY CLASS FOR ART. HE'LL MAKE A GOOD JOB OF THEM!
THERE! ISN'T THAT A MASTERPIECE, JIMMY?
IT CERTAINLY IS! BEND DOWN A LITTLE SO I CAN SEE IT BETTER, DICK.
SURE.
YOU ASKED FOR IT, DICK!
HO-HO-HO!
KICK ME HARD
THUD!
OOYAH!
BAH! THAT WAS A DIRTY ROTTEN TRICK TO PLAY ON ME!
HO-HO!
HA-HA!
HEY, WAIT A MINUTE, THOUGH! I MIGHT BE ABLE TO USE THESE TRANSFERS TO TATTOO MYSELF!
TRANSFERS
IN THE SHOP
GOSH! THERE'S MACHINERY WORKING BEHIND THAT DOOR. IT MUST BE A PRINTING PRESS!
MUM-M BUZZ
PRINTING DEPT
I'LL SNEAK IN AND SEE IF I CAN GET SOMETHING PRINTED ON MY SKIN.
PRINTING DEPT
TWO MINUTES LATER
GET OUT—AND STAY OUT!
PRINTING DEPT
BIFF!
YOWCH!
HI, FOLKS! I TRIED TO GET A TATTOO FROM A PRINTING MACHINE, BUT I - ER - GOT A BIT BLOTTED!
STOP PRESS
DAILY CRO
GASP!
THAT'S THE KIND OF TATTOO DICK DESERVES! DAD'S GIVING IT TO HIM—WITH A SLIPPER!
THUD! THUD! THUD! THUD!
OW! WOW! OOYAH!

RIBBONSDAY

WHAT A LOAD OF GIRLS IN OUR STREET—AND ALL WITH SILLY RIBBONS IN THEIR HAIR! BUT NOT FOR LONG!

BULLY BEEF and CHIPS

PULL!
JERK!
OUCH!
OOYAH!

YEOWW!
TUG!

HO-HO! I'VE GOT DOZENS OF RIBBONS NOW!
AND I KNOW WHAT TO DO WITH 'EM!

THEY MAKE A SMASHING LASSO!
WOW!

COME HERE AND GET THUMPED, CHIPS!
OOYAH!
PULL!

LOOK, GIRLS! THERE ARE OUR RIBBONS! LET'S RUSH HIM!
OH, GOSH!

HOW DARE YOU STEAL OUR RIBBONS? TAKE THAT!
OUCH!
SOCK!
THIEF!
GIMME THOSE BACK!
PULL!

HO-HO! THAT SAVED ME THE BOTHER OF BASHING YOU AGAIN!
BAH!

I DIDN'T PINCH YOUR RIBBONS. IT WAS BULLY BEEF! WILL YOU HELP ME GET OUR OWN BACK?
OKAY, CHIPS!

DON'T LET BULLY BEEF SEE YOUR PONY TAIL, ELSIE, OR HE'LL PINCH YOUR RIBBON!

HO-HO! CHIPS WAS DEAD RIGHT!
PULL!

OOYAH!
'60s

HO-HO! BEEFY DIDN'T KNOW ELSIE WAS A PONY!
HURRY, GERTIE! PUT THE ROPE ON BEFORE HE COMES ROUND!

HO-HO! BEEFY'S CLOTHES WILL BE IN RIBBONS BEFORE LONG!
OUCH! OOYAH! HELP!
BUMP!
SCRAPE!

THIRSTDAY THE Dandy

3d.

EVERY TUESDAY. No. 1206—JAN, 2nd. 1965.

2.1.65

FLYDAY

Desperate DAN

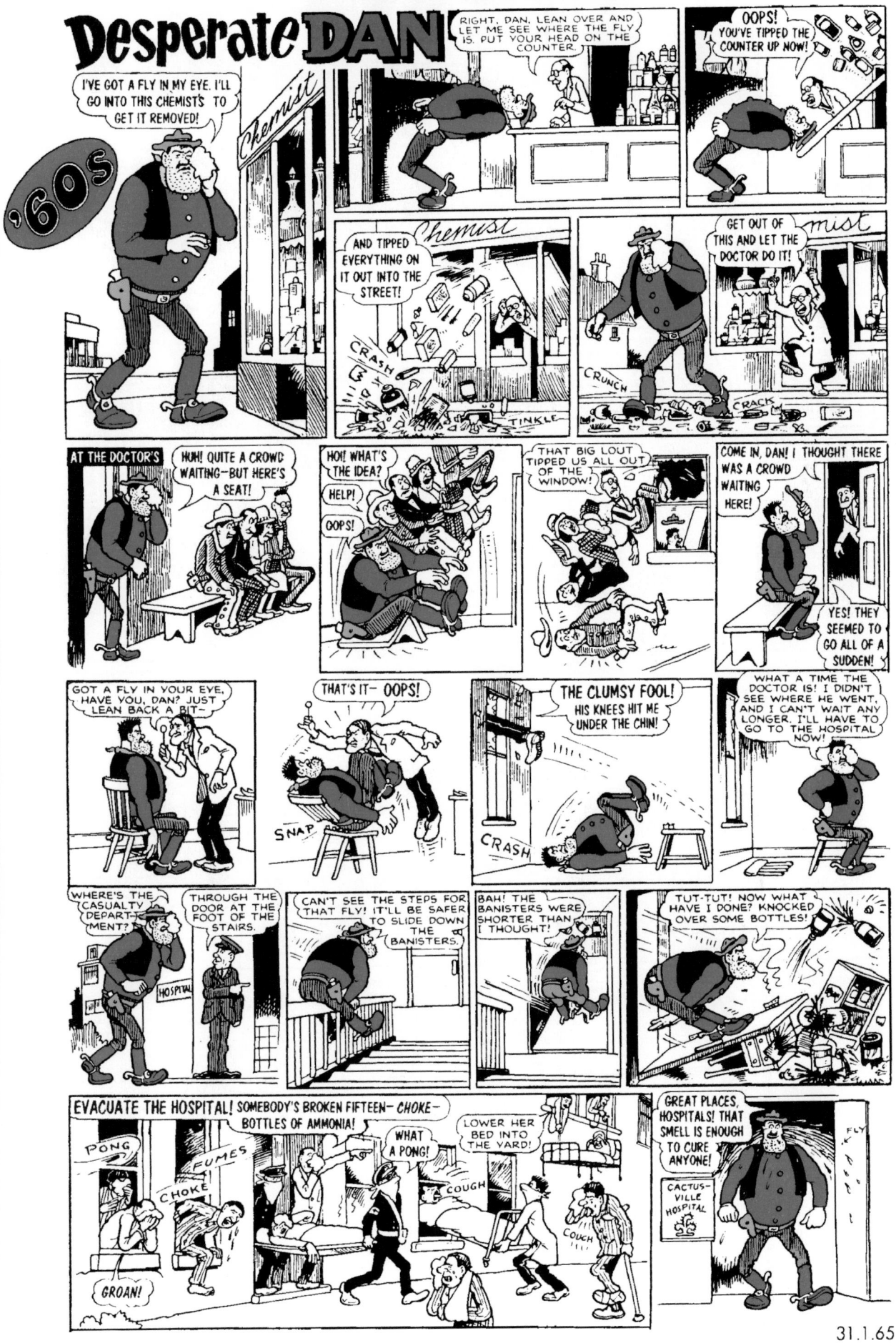

31.1.65

SPLATDIRTDAY

Just a couple of years ago someone came up with the idea of a washing machine for dogs, where the dog is sprayed with water in a large metal container, complete with window, so the dog can keep an eye on his owner! Well, the idea isn't so new after all, as this Biffo The Bear from 1969 demonstrates — although Professor Screwtopp's machine doesn't have a window!

A story set in the 18th century, from a Beano of the 20th century,

RED RORY OF THE EAGLES

IT is the 18th of April, 1746. Bonnie Prince Charlie and his Highland Army have been routed at the Battle of Culloden and are now hunted high and low by the Redcoat soldiers . . . Young Red Rory Macpherson and his magnificent golden eagles, Flame and Fury, have been given the task of driving a small herd of Highland cattle to Sir Donald Stuart of Lochornhead many miles to the west. For some reason, unknown to Rory, the safe delivery of these beasts can mean life or death for Prince Charlie. But, to his horror, the lad finds that the cattle have been taken by the Redcoats to provide their army with fresh meat . . .

reproduced in the 21st century!

26.5.62

This forty-year-old story from The Dandy is a

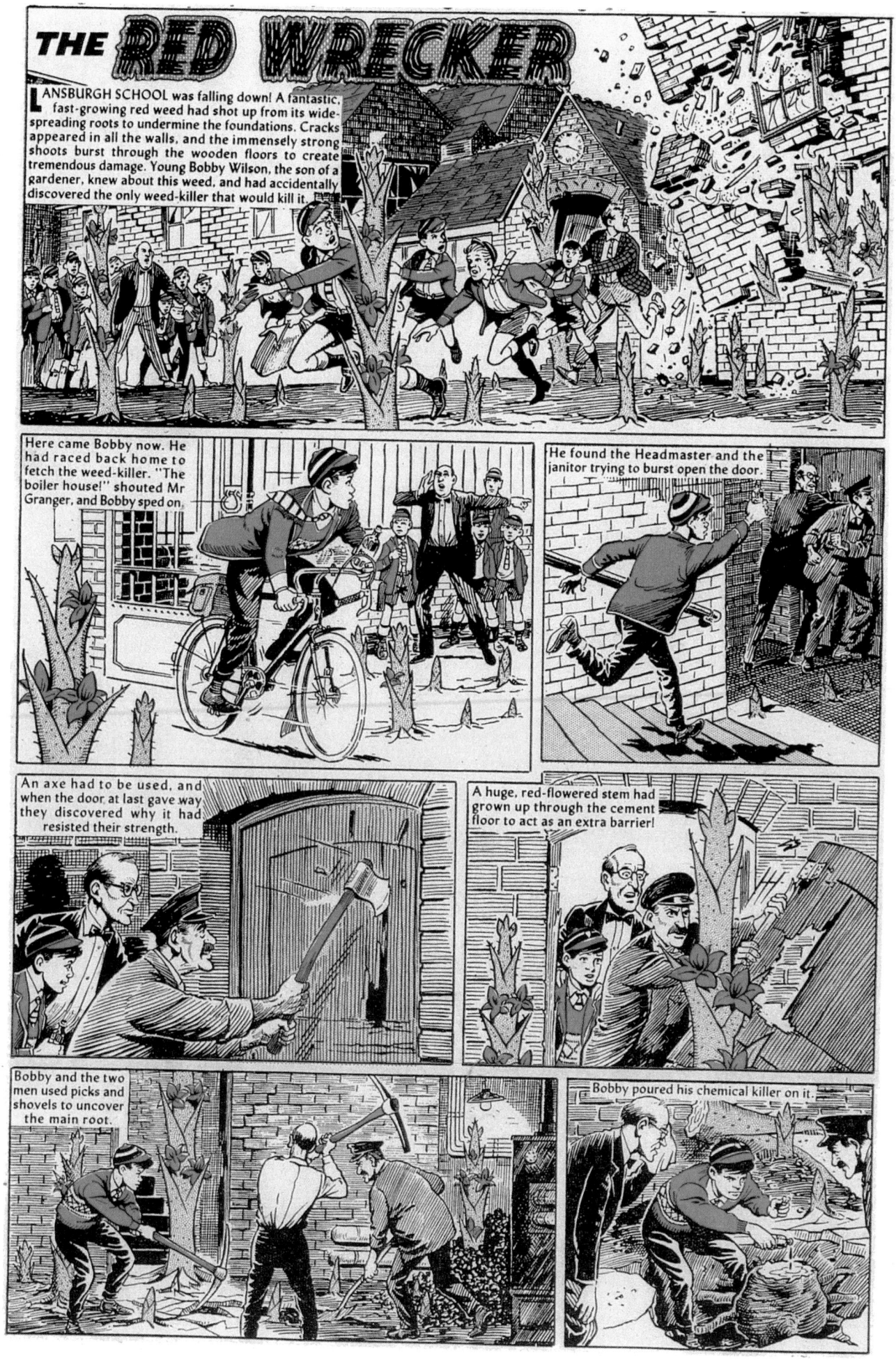

cautionary tale to all growers of hybrid plants . . .

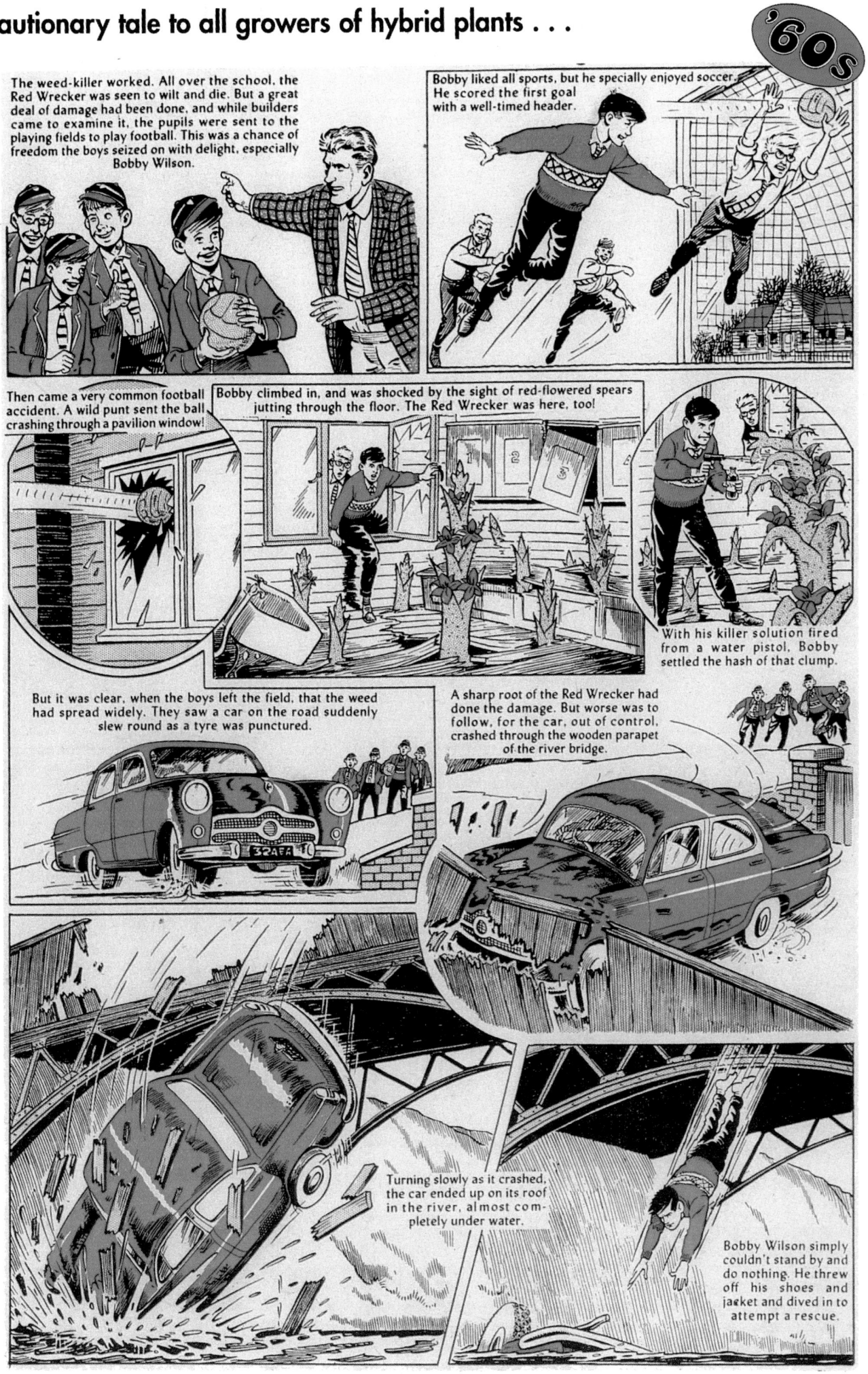

It took almost all the boy's strength to haul the drowning man from inside.
His school pals were ready to help, and they tried to revive the unconscious driver.
ROAD WORK
While Bobby dried his clothes by a fire where two men were digging for a root of the Red Wrecker, he suddenly thought of something that had to be done at once.
Racing home, he entered the garden shed. He was going to burn up that packet of foreign seed that had given birth to the Red Wrecker.
The seeds were gone! Bobby was completely puzzled. Who had taken them? And why?
Down at the river that night, a man who had very nearly been drowned returned to the scene of his accident. He groped inside the crashed car.
When he waded towards the bank again, the mystery man was pocketing a square package taken from the car.
In the middle of the night a week later Bobby Wilson was awakened by Constable Carstairs, who knew that the red weed had first appeared in the Wilson garden. "Look!" he said at the river bank. Bobby stared in horror. The sunken car could be seen again, borne upwards on the thrusting stems of the Red Wrecker!
JEW
And down at a jeweller's store in Lansburgh a shadowy figure watched more red shoots thrusting up through the pavement! It was he who had sown some seeds here!

20.9.64

The vehicle in this 'odd-ball' story was described as "a tank without caterpillar tracks" and "an armoured car without wheels" but Dandy readers in 1963/64 knew it as . . .

The Crimson Ball

TWO farmhands stared in wonder at the great red Ball that revolved in the duck-pond. They had read about it in the newspapers, of course. This was the mystery invader known as the Crimson Ball. It had been set on fire by a boy called Peter Jones, and now it was cooling down.

Now the Master of the Crimson Ball seemed to be in a fury. The Ball came hurtling after the boy, who had reached the rear door of a cinema. In sheer desperation, he burst the door open.

But he had barely got inside and turned from the side passage to the middle one when the Crimson Ball came after him—bursting through a brick wall and through the cinema screen to get at him!

The audience panicked, screaming in fear as each and every one scrambled to get out of the way. Seats were buckled and crushed as the Crimson Ball pursued Peter.

Peter reached the open air only a few yards ahead. Turning, he threw his last bottle of chemical mixture. If this one didn't work, his number was up.

But, wonder of wonders! The Crimson Ball burst into flames as the bottle shattered against it! Peter's heart leapt. He had found the stuff that would destroy the Ball!

Almost at once hope turned to despair, for several well-meaning citizens sprang to action. There was danger that the burning Ball would set the whole street ablaze, so two men turned fire extinguishers on it, while another phoned for help.

"No! Let it burn!" yelled Peter frantically.

The men wouldn't listen to him. In a few minutes the fire brigade was at work, reeling out hoses and playing jets on the burning Crimson Ball. In sheer desperation, Peter ran towards a fire engine to stop the firemen's work.

Snatching a fireman's axe, Peter sprang to the nearest line of hose and cleaved it clean through. An angry fireman leaped to grab him.

There was still a chance, Peter thought. He wriggled free.

He pelted off towards the smoking hot Crimson Ball.

This time Peter was after the broken bottle. On its label were details of the chemicals which had set the Ball on fire, and Peter must get it to restart the blaze.

Now the Ball came rolling after its chief enemy, the boy who knew the secret of how to set it on fire.

When Peter slipped through a fence and crossed the main road, the Crimson Ball caused havoc amongst the traffic. A lorry was knocked spinning and a car crashed into it. Another car slewed into a ditch to avoid the Ball. Peter ran on, clutching his bottle.

When a canvas-roofed lorry passed him, the boy took a desperate chance. He tossed the broken bottle on to its roof.

Before the Crimson Ball could overtake the lorry, a canal bridge opened to let a barge through. Foiled, the Ball went after Peter again. But he had in the meantime taken his chance to write a note to the police.

In the main street of the little town, as the Crimson Ball approached, Peter hurled a stone through a jeweller's window. His note was tied to it—and this was Peter's way of making sure the police got his message.

But now he was at the mercy of the Crimson Ball. It was right on his heels—and presently it gave him his orders.

"Lead the way to Farnbury Aerodrome," commanded the Master. "Try any tricks and you'll be crushed to death!"

'60s
Even forty years ago, people wanted special features in their gardens — but the one that Dennis the Menace's dad wants wouldn't go "down well" nowadays!
WONDER WHAT THE MAN-NEXT-DOOR'S DOIN'?
LATER—
I'LL GIVE HIM A SALVO— PUFF!
LOT O' FLIES ABOUT, TODAY!
I SEE ONE INSECT I'D LIKE TO SWAT —YOU!
WHOOSH!
GURGLE
GOSH! HE'S MAKIN' A SWIMMIN' POOL! I MUST GET MY BATHIN' TRUNKS.
BAH! IT'S THE MENACE AGAIN.
YIPPEE—GLUG!
I BUILT THIS POOL SPECIALLY FOR MY PRIZE GOLDFISH. YOU'LL STAY OUT OF IT, SEE?
YAH! OL' SPOILSPORT!
THEN—
LOVELY DAY FOR FISHIN'!
AGH! HE'S TRYIN' TO CATCH MY PRECIOUS FISHIES!
KEEP THIS BOY UNDER CONTROL, OR ELSE!
TOSS
THEN—
COO! GOOD OL' DAD'S MAKIN' A SWIMMIN' POOL FOR ME!
WHEN ARE YOU GONNA PUT THE WATER IN IT, DAD?
I'M NOT GOING TO PUT WATER IN IT—
—I'M GOING TO PUT YOU IN IT!
GOOD SHOW!
WOW!
THIS PIT MAKES AN IDEAL, NON-ESCAPE PLAY-PEN FOR A CHILD LIKE DENNIS!
HERE'S A NICE STALE BUN FOR YOU, LADDIE!
SNARL!

DO NOT make your own stink bombs!

DO NOT steal gas cylinders!

DO NOT use a blowtorch!

DO NOT try to be a burglar!

DO NOT use a brazier for cooking!

DO NOT touch gas meters!

DO NOT touch electricity!

DO NOT strike a match if there's a gas leak!

That's all the warnings over! Now sit back and enjoy this Winker Watson story from the Dandy 1969.

Winker passed out heaps of grub, and he didn't seem to mind that most of it was raw.
BUT, WINKER, ALL THIS STUFF NEEDS COOKING!
DON'T WORRY. I'VE THOUGHT OF THAT, TOO!
The workmen didn't ask where the stuff came from. They just sat back and enjoyed it!
JOLLY NICE OF YOU GAS BLOKES TO LET US COOK ON YOUR BRAZIER! YOU MUST TUCK IN WITH US!
STEAK AND CHIPS NEXT FOR TWO, WINKER.
RATHER, SON, IT'S BETTER THAN SANDWICHES!
GAS COMPANY
LATER - BACK AT GREYTOWERS
HOLD IT, EVERYBODY! THE CREEPS ARE HEADING FOR THE PANTRY WINDOW! LET'S HIDE AND KEEP AN EYE ON 'EM!
Winker had a feeling that the Creeps were up to something.
Winker was right! Creepy's sister was Headmistress of Oak Lodge, and she was just as big a skinflint as her brother.
WE'LL BE ABLE TO COOK THIS LATER, AGNES. THE WORKMEN SAY THE GAS WILL BE ON TONIGHT, BUT I WON'T TELL THE BOYS—THEY CAN MAKE DO WITH SALADS AGAIN!
I'LL COOK US A YUMMY SUPPER, CLARENCE!
THAT NIGHT -
GRR! IT'S NOT FAIR! THE CREEPS ARE COOKING LOVELY GRUB FOR THEMSELVES AND WE GET NONE! COME ON, TROTTY, DOWN TO THE CELLAR WE GO, AND WE'LL PUT PAID TO THEIR LITTLE GAME!
KITCHEN WASTE
Winker didn't have much time to cook up a scheme, but it was easy to stop the Creeps cooking!
If Winker and his pals couldn't get a hot meal, then neither should the Creeps!
THERE! I'VE TURNED OFF THE GAS AT THE MAIN, AND IT SERVES THEM JOLLY WELL RIGHT!
ON
OFF
GAS METER
The mouths of the Creeps were watering when things began to go wrong for them.
EEEK! OO, CLARENCE, THE GAS HAS GONE OUT!
OH, BOTHER! I'LL JUST CHECK THE MAIN TAP IN THE CELLAR, AGNES!
PHUT!
Down in the cellar, Creepy was mystified.
OHO, THAT'S FUNNY! THE SUPPLY WAS SHUT OFF! I'LL TURN IT ON AGAIN AND TELL AGNES WHAT HAPPENED.
ON
OFF
GAS METER
He was no sooner back upstairs, however, than Winker did something else to harass him.
YOO-HOO, AGNES, THE GAS IS ON AGAIN ..... EEEK! NOW THE LIGHTS HAVE GONE OUT!
DON'T PANIC, AGNES! I'LL JUST STRIKE A MATCH AND SEE WHERE I'M GOING .....
This was the silliest thing Creepy could have done! Wait for it!
WHOOSH! BANG!
OO-ER! I FORGOT TO TURN OFF THE GAS TAPS!
h, boy! Creepy had done it now. He had shattered the kitchen!
NEXT DAY
Ha-ha! The boys would eat well for the next week until the kitchen was repaired—but Creepy wouldn't! He'd be broke after paying for all the meals!
ER, WE'RE FROM GREYTOWERS SCHOOL, AND WE'LL BE HAVING ALL OUR MEALS HERE FOR A WEEK—AND THE HEADMASTER SAYS THAT—SNIFF!— YOU'RE TO SEND THE BILL TO—SNIFF! SNIFF!— CLARENCE AND AGNES CREEP!
MANAGER
RITZ Hotel
DINING ROOM

23.8.69

There was 'thumping' wild about Beano characters Punch and Jimmy —

they argued and bashed lumps out of each other for five years between 1962 and 1967.
Huh! Nothing to fight about!
Hey! I've got an idea– I'll say something, and you disagree!
Super! That's bound to start a fight!
SO–
I LIKE "THE BEANO"! WHAT ARE YOU GOING TO DO ABOUT IT?
COME ON! PUT THEM UP!
I can't – I like "The Beano" as well!
Look – I'll say something and YOU disagree.
Ok!
SO–
I DON'T LIKE HOMEWORK!
But I don't like it either!
G-golly! If we agree on everything, we'll never be able to fight again!
Ah-ha! We must make sure they ALWAYS agree!
SO–
I'll just tell Punch he's got an ugly face – he'll disagree with that!
Oh-oh!
PUNCH! YOU'VE GOT AN....
....ugly face! Gulp!
SO I HAVE!
LATER–
Jimmy won't agree if I say he's got hair like a bed of weeds!
JIMMY, YOU'VE GOT HAIR LIKE A BED OF WEEDS – C-CRUMBS!
BUT, AFTER TWO HOURS OF MAKING SURE THE TWINS AGREE–
Heh! Heh! Mum and Dad are worn out!
I agree about that too!
19.12.67

DENNIS THE MENACE
CLEANER . . . DENNIS . . . just for once these two words go together, in this 1962 tale — proving that vacuums aren't just for "suckers"!
BAH! I CAN'T READ MY "BEANO" FOR THE NOISE THAT THING'S MAKING.
The Beano
WHINE!
SUCK!
SLUP!
SLURP!
SUCK!
WHIRR!
THIS'LL BE A LAUGH!
SNAKE
WHEE!
SUCK!
WHINE!
ACHOO!
WHEE!
ACHOO!
EEK!
HAW! HAW!
LATER—
HEH-HEH! I'LL BORROW MUM'S CLEANER AND HAVE SOME MORE FUN!
60s
COME ON, SUCKER!
TUT-TUT! THERE'S SOME NASTY YELLOW DUST ON DAD'S PRIZE ROSE. I'D BETTER REMOVE IT.
OOPS! I'VE OVER-DONE IT!
WHEE!
SUCK!
BALD
SUCK!
THAT POOR OLD CHAP'S TEA'S TOO HOT. I'LL JUST SWITCH THE MACHINE TO "BLOW" AND—
—HOW'S THAT, SIR?
BLAST
THEN—
I'M GOING TO GIVE THIS LOLLY A GOOD BIG SUCK. SLURP!
SUCK!
CACKLE! BUT NOT IF I SUCK IT FIRST, WALTER! TA!
EEK!
WHAT ARE YOU UP TO, DENNIS?
TIME I WAS OFF!
BUT—
MUM! FETCH MY SLIPPER!
SUCK!

There's no need to get yourself in a tangle like Korky! It's very easy to order your favourite comics so you never miss an issue — just take out a year's subscription to The Beano or The Dandy by applying for details online at:—
www.beanotown.com
(Please quote DBAS06 when placing your order.)
Or contact us by phoning the following numbers (No, Korky won't be connecting you!):—
Subscription Freephone No.— 0800 318846 (UK only)
Overseas Direct Line — +44 1382 575582
Or you can write to us at the following address:—
Subscribers' Department, D. C. Thomson & Co. Ltd., 80 Kingsway East, Dundee, DD4 8SL.

13.8.66
COO! LOOK AT THAT!
'60s
HERE'S A "MITE"Y FUNNY STORY FOR ALL MICROSCOPIC MENACE FANS!